heavenly

A HUNDRED YEARS OF UNFORGETTABLE WOMEN

DONALD F. REUTER

UNIVERSE PUBLISHING

creative direction and design by Donald F. Reuter for **alias** BOOKS

First published in the United States
of America in 1999
by UNIVERSE PUBLISHING
A Division of Rizzoli International
Publications, Inc.
300 Park Avenue South
New York, NY 10010

©1999 Donald F. Reuter and

alias
BOOKS

99 00 01 02 / 10 9 8 7 6 5 4 3 2 1

ISBN: 0-7893-0377-9

Printed in China

—To all the wonderful
women entertainers who
watched over me and kept
me from harm while I was
growing up (and they really
did)—who taught me
about style and culture,
laughter and how to cry
(both of which I did often),
sadness and love, reality
and fantasy. Even today I
look to them for help, and
they always answer uncon-
ditionally. I hope in some
way this book begins to
repay my debt.

front cover

G E N E   T I E R N E Y

Born November 20, 1920, in Brooklyn, New York. Died 1991
Discovered by Darryl F. Zanuck, Tierney became one of his studio's top stars of the '40s
and into the '50s. She was most memorable in three films, *Laura* (1944), *Leave Her to
Heaven* (1945), and *The Ghost and Mrs. Muir* (1947). Though her beauty is near-classic, it is
renowned for its distinguishing features: almond-shaped eyes, pronounced cheekbones,
and an imperceptible overbite (which gave even her sharpest moments onscreen a touch
of humility). Married once to designer Oleg Cassini (from 1941 to 1952), she was also
linked, romantically, to Aly Khan (after Rita Hayworth), and John F. Kennedy (before his
presidency). (*Everett*)

endpapers

J O A N   C R A W F O R D

L u c i l l e   F a y   L e S u e u r
Born March 23, 1904, in San Antonio, Texas. Died 1977
Easily one of the most versatile and long-lived of film resumes Joan's career spanned an
amazing five decades. Now as famous as the mother-to-end-all-mothers, Crawford's
steely determination and stamina is itself possible reason for some measure of forgive-
ness for her alleged shortcomings. Pick your favorite persona: smart-assed flapper, Adri-
an-tailored career gal, jaded heroine, woman with a past, or maniacal matron—she played
them all with great aplomb. With a list of film credits that could become a phone book, if
one had to choose a cinematic highlight the selection would invariably lead to her stellar
role of Mildred Pierce, in the film of the same name from 1945 (a career apex that falls
neatly into the middle of her reign). This is where you really get a chance to see star
power in all its glory. (*Kobal*)

opener

D I A H A N N   C A R R O L L

Born July 17, 1935, in the Bronx, New York
Blessed with a serene beauty and crystalline singing voice, Carroll was only in her early
twenties when she first appeared on Broadway (*House of Flowers*) and on film (*Carmen
Jones*, 1954). She became a Tony winner in 1962 for her lead role in Rodgers and Hammerstein's *No Strings*; a highlight, her rendition of the song, "The Sweetest Sound." Went
into television history books as the star of her landmark comedy series, "Julia" (1968-
–71). Though it was not the first show to feature a black female star, that honor goes to
"Beulah" (1951–53), there would be no comparing the two in terms of lead character
representation; "Beulah" was based on a domestic, "Julia" a working professional. Back
on film, she was nominated for an Oscar for *Claudine* (1974). Memorably joined the cast
of TV's "Dynasty," as Dominique Devereux during the 1983–84 season. (*Gene
Howard/MPTV*)

title page

P I E R   A N G E L I

A n n a   M a r i a   P i e r a n g e l i
Born June 19, 1932, in Cagliari, Sardinia, Italy. Died 1971
Fawnlike and fragile, Angeli's delicate screen presence belied a volatile and erratic off
camera existence. Married twice, including to singer Vic Damone (from 1954–58), as well
as a highly publicized affair with James Dean, Pier's life ended in suicide, at the age of thir-
ty-nine, from an overdose of barbituates. Twin sister of fellow actress Marisa Pavan, Pier's
first American film was Fred Zinnemann's *Teresa* (1951). Best known movie: *Somebody Up
There Likes Me* (1956) with Paul Newman. (*Corbis-Bettmann*)

right

A N N E T T E   F U N I C E L L O

Born October 22, 1942, in Utica, New York
First a Mouseketeer, then the one-piece swimsuit-attired object of our affections in a
drove of meaningless, yet enjoyable, beach party flicks, often with Frankie Avalon, then
more recently, a peanut butter spokesperson. This most adorable female of boyhood
crushes also enjoyed a handful of finger-popping Top-40 music hits, including "Pineapple
Princess" (1960). Today is valiantly struggling with the debilitating effects of advanced
multiple sclerosis. (*Corbis-Bettmann*)

Throughout *Heavenly* I was fortunate to be given the opportunity to include the thoughts and comments of a select group of women who appear within its pages. Though the gathering may seem arbitrary to some, this was not the case. Each individual, on some level great or minute, whether through style, humor, or controversy, touched and influenced my life. That I was able to speak with each one at great length and with much ease was an amazing display of their generosity. I would like to express my most heartfelt thanks and appreciation to them for their priceless contribution.

leslie caron • **rosemary clooney**

angie dickinson • *celeste holm*

shirley jones • *nancy kwan*

janet leigh • *liza minnelli*

rita moreno • *kim novak*

paula prentiss • *gena rowlands*

brooke shields • *esther williams*

vanessa williams

contributors

JANE FONDA

Born December 21, 1937, in New York City In more or less the following order: daughter of famed actor, Henry; first notable acting job, in 1954, opposite said-father in a community theater production of *The Country Girl*; attended Vassar; left for Paris to study art; formal dramatic training at The Actor's Studio; Broadway and Hollywood debuts, 1960; more movies; married Roger Vadim (late of Bardot) in 1965; ever more movies; cult fave *Barbarella* (via Vadim) in 1968; became political antiwar activist, late-'60s; dubbed "Hanoi Jane"; first Oscar nom, 1969, for *They Shoot Horses, Don't They?*; first Oscar, *Klute* (1971); marries Tom Hayden, 1973; third nomination, for *Julia*, 1977; second Oscar, for *Coming Home*, 1978 (three more noms to follow); appears with father in *On Golden Pond*, 1981; becomes fitness enthusiast and aerobic guru to millions, making millions; officially becomes politician's wife, 1982; divorces Hayden, 1990; becomes tycoon's wife (Ted Turner), 1991; retires from acting shortly thereafter; mid-'90s, seen doing notorious "Tomahawk Chop" at Atlanta Braves game with then-owner hubby; late-'90s, living the good life in Montana and thereabouts. Whew! and she still looks amazing. (*Archive Photos*)

It was necessary to place the women of *Heavenly* into separate categories; my only other option was to alphabetize them—how boring! However, their placement is not random, and just because you find someone in one section does not mean they wouldn't fit just as nicely (or better) in another. Nevertheless, I had my own reasons for putting them where they are (although there will be some who will disagree with the results).

STELLA STEVENS
Estelle Egglestone
Born October 1, 1936, in Hot Coffee, Mississippi
Combining virtuousness with sex appeal, Stevens was a popular actress, albeit never a top star. Her busy career got off to a fine start with *L'il Abner* (1959) as Appassionata von Climax, the same year she was given a Golden Globe for Most Promising Actress. But from that point on her film work was rarely alleviated by the type of vehicle that would command more of her than just her good looks. By 1980, she tried her hand at directing and in the late '90s became a published novelist. Mother of actor Andrew Stevens. (*Archive Photos*)

Contents

When I was fourteen, I remember my ninth grade teacher asking our class, "What do you want to be when you grow up?" Everyone had a typical answer: a doctor, a lawyer, an athlete, someone even wanted to be a millionaire (I was all for that, too!). When she eventually got around to me, I spilled forth, "I want to be the first guy to win three Best Actor Oscars (secretly wanting to match Katharine Hepburn's then-record three—she has since added a fourth)." Flummoxed, and with no response that I can recall, she went on to the next eager young charge. Unperturbed, the moment stuck in my head, but not because of my instructor's indifference. No, I was amazed (it took so little) that I had such a specific future planned for myself. Now it goes without saying that the "goal" was not reached (not yet, anyway). But over the years I came to understand why I felt so strongly that that was what I thought I was going to do in the first place. Entertainers (not just actors from movies, mind you) meant everything to me as an awkward, isolated kid in Cincinnati, Ohio. Culturally, since I was half-German, half-Korean, I was automatically separated from my Appalachian neighbors, and furthermore, I was not good in sports, considered "artistic," liked to sing (mostly alone with my soundtrack records), and was skinny *and* a "four-eyes." Yikes! So I escaped into a world of fantasy, typically via whatever was playing on the family television (or the one in my room). It could have been a seventies sitcom, black-and-white film *noir*, a Mitzi Gaynor variety special, or a David Lean epic—I loved them all. Nor did this steady stream of fluff and stuff come just from the "box." Occasionally, the family would go out to a film (usually a Disney flick—*Jungle Book* was a fave). Neither was my affinity for them totally singular—besides the millions who obviously share my enthusiasm, my mother, being an enormous movie fan herself, reinforced the validity of my affection.

prelude

left

MARION DAVIES
Marion Cecilia Douras
Born January 3, 1897, in Brooklyn, New York. Died 1961
Sometimes you can try too hard. Possibly if William Randolph Hearst had stayed out of the picture, a bright, talented, and cheerful Davies would have enjoyed the type of career that he had so valiantly strove to acquire for her (including going so far as to create an entire film studio, Cosmopolitan, for her productions). His attempts did make her famous, but never a success at the box office (mainly because the pictures could not recoup the lavish budgets he imposed upon them). Though their relationship was famously (though not accurately) memorialized in the classic *Citizen Kane* (1941), in reality they shared a wonderful, lifelong relationship (until Hearst's death in 1951). The two would have married had Mrs. Hearst ever consented to a divorce. Once Davies retired from films in 1937—partially because of the Hearst's financial misfortunes and partially because she did not do well in talkies (she tended to stutter)—she parlayed her own considerable wealth (which she smartly accumulated throughout the salad years) into a profession as a successful business executive. (*Author's collection*)

right

DORIS DAY
Doris Von Kappelhoff
Born April 3, 1924, in Cincinnati, Ohio
Appearing unflappable and cheery, Doris' real life was far from the candy-colored existence she so effortlessly sold to her adoring fans. From early debilitating illness to bad marriages and financial destitution (especially when she should have been reaping the rewards of hard-earned wealth), Day never let her fans suffer from her misfortunes. An accomplished band singer in the '40s, she got a film break in 1948 (replacing Betty Hutton) in *Romance on the High Seas*. By the early '60s, she was the country's top star (female or male) and redefined the comic heroine, with an uncanny sense of timing and delivery, in a series of bedroom farces (*Pillow Talk*, 1959, and her only Oscar nom) that she could pretty much call her own. This freckle-faced darling was also responsible for making popular two Oscar-winning songs, "Secret Love" (from *Calamity Jane*, 1953) and "Que Sera, Sera" (from *The Man Who Knew Too Much*, 1956). (*Archive Photos*)

GWYNETH PALTROW
Born September 28, 1972, in Los Angeles, California
The latest addition into the Hollywood firmament. Daughter of actress Blythe Danner and producer/director Bruce Paltrow, Gwyneth showed early signs of true acting talent, but did not break through until *Emma* in 1996. Her elegant demeanor and looks recall both Grace Kelly and Audrey Hepburn, with enough contemporary verve to satisfy modern audiences, as is evident in her resplendent Oscar-winning role in *Shakespeare in Love* (1999). The part and her still-new career is a perfect way to close this century's starry legacy with abundant promise for the future. (*Berliner Studio/Corbis-Outline*)

As I grew older, I began to fully comprehend why I liked *male* movie stars, like Tab Hunter and Montgomery Clift, but I honestly didn't like most of the other guys—they were so earnest, forthright, and dull! I gravitated much more easily to the dames. Their plights seemed more tragic and heroic; their victories, more deserved (their outfits, so much prettier!). So, after careful analysis, I realized (as an impressionable teenager) it was not so surprising that I wanted to earn the same awards as Madame Hepburn; she was *my* role model—the same way a star athlete would be to someone else.

So, I came up with *Heavenly* as my way of honoring all those lovely, inspiring women. But I don't want to mislead you into thinking that this is a complete gathering of the most unforgettable women of the last one hundred years. It is not. For one thing, you must consider the physical limitations. How many individuals could I cram into one book before the whole enterprise began to look ridiculous? For another, I was looking at this project as an emotionally pleasing (admittedly, my own)—not intellectual—endeavor. So, as a matter of course, I chose first from my heart. However, I did want this to be as democratic a gathering as possible, so I made everyone on my initial list (of women) go through four rites of passage: One, was the individual someone I had to include or risk being censured? (like Garbo, Dietrich, etc.); Two, was she a woman I loved more than life itself? (Sorry, I will not name names—you'll just have to guess who they are); Three (and possibly the most important), was her photo *nice*, or interesting, colorful, rarely or never seen, or—not to forget—one that I could get my hands on without paying a bloody fortune? (Point three got more unusual choices included in the book than it kept people out.); Finally, four, would their inclusion trigger a reaction—good, bad, or indifferent? Considering the very subjective nature of this point, I may never completely know the answer to that one. It is also the main reason why there is an obvious absence of many current favorites—you see them all the time, anyway—and the inclusion of some more obscure selections. Once you run each lady through all four obstacles, you begin to understand why Connie Stevens is included and Jessica Lange is not. At least, I hope so. (Incidentally, I love both of them.)

Once the selection process was completed (and it was changing up to the very last minute), I had to then place their pictures somewhere in the book. So I came up with categories and named them. This is where things got even more dicey. When you do a book about men, like our companion publication *Heartthrob*, you can have a bit of fun labelling the guys; because after all, they're men and they can take it. (Ahem.) But do the same thing with a book on women, and the whole thing takes on an unintentional sexist edge. But, you know what? I couldn't please everybody (nor do I offend, without reason). Therefore, I went ahead and gave these sections names that, on the one hand were to be expected, or on the other may seem dated, chauvinist, or thoughtless. For instance, neither "blondie" nor "sugar & spice" could be thought of as particularly endearing today, though they are not outrightly offensive. However, in this context, they serve a somewhat subliminal purpose; they make you think about how we categorize and label as a matter of course. And that's as deep as I will get on the subject, I promise.

A few things before I leave you to *Heavenly*: This is not a reference guide and should not be thought of as one. I am not an authority on the subject of "unforgettable" women, at least no more or less than anyone else, but I did try to include as much relevant information as possible. Given names were added when I had them available and only if they were significantly different from chosen ones. The comments gathered from my cherished contributors were written two different ways—as direct quotes and essays—based mainly on the individual's preference. The photographs were not dated because the accuracy of the information could not be verified in enough instances to be consistent (the same with birthdates). Awards, nominations, and other distinctions of merit were mentioned only arbitrarily—their listings are not complete unless noted.

clockwise, from far left

B E B E   D A N I E L S

Born January 14, 1901, in Dallas, Texas. Died 1971
At one time, Daniels was one of the silent screen's biggest stars, but like so many others her popularity waned with the coming of sound. Surprisingly, it was not because of her voice (in fact, she was a fine singer, too) or talent. But, unexplicably, audiences looked to fresher faces and her film career never recovered. So, making the most of a bad situation, Daniels and her husband, actor Ben Lyon, took an engagement at the London Palladium and moved. Once there, they included radio in their repertoire and became enormously successful, ending up one of the medium's most popular on-air couples. (*Kobal*)

L I L L I A N   G I S H

Born October 14, 1896, in Springfield, Ohio. Died 1993
The First Lady of the Silent Screen. As an actress, Gish took her work very seriously and helped make motion pictures into a respected medium. Her work with acclaimed director D. W. Griffith, including *Birth of a Nation* (1915), *Intolerance* (1916), and *Broken Blossoms* (1918), revolutionized filmmaking. Occasionally returning to films after her retirement in 1930, Gish was nominated for a Supporting Actress Oscar in 1946, for *A Duel in the Sun*. Her 100th film was Altman's *A Wedding* (1978), her last: *Whales of August* (1987). (*Kobal*)

T H E D A   B A R A

Theodosia   Goodman
Born July 29, 1890, in Cincinnati, Ohio. Died 1955
Today's film "realism" makes it hard to comprehend the popularity of many of the greatest stars of the Silent Era. A perfect example is Theda Bara, who, by today's standards, appears almost otherworldly. But don't let her over-painted, man-hungry facade fool you. During the period of her greatest popularity (around 1914–19) she was a sensation. Named "the Vamp," even her humble beginnings (she was the daughter of a tailor) were corrupted to match her onscreen, vampirish demeanor; she was turned into the love-child of a French artist and his Egyptian mistress. However, her career could not stand the excess, and by the '20s she was through in Hollywood, retiring completely in 1926. (*Kobal*)

M A R Y   P I C K F O R D

Gladys   Smith
Born April 8, 1893, in Toronto, Canada. Died 1979
Ironic that the screen's most popular star would still herald from the Silent Era. But in Pickford's time, she commanded studios, directors, and audiences alike with a velvet-gloved iron hand. Some numbers: she started out in 1909 making $40 a week, by 1917 the sum was $350,000 a picture. But fame came at a professional price; having acquired the title "America's Sweetheart" her fans demanded she play nothing but virtuous little girls. Gifted in the boardroom, too, Pickford formed, with Charlie Chaplin, D. W. Griffith, and Douglas Fairbanks, United Artists. She was to marry Fairbanks, and with him become Hollywood's most adored couple; their home was the legendary Pickfair. By 1929, with the emergence of talkies, Pickford, in a daring move, played a "modern" in *Coquette*. It resulted in an Oscar-winning performance. However, sound films proved elusive, and she made only a few more before her retirement, in 1933. (*Kobal*)

right

A L L A   N A Z I M O V A

Born June 4, 1879, in Yalta, Crimea, Russia. Died 1945
Nazimova was considered to be one of the early century's most gifted stage actresses, having trained under Stanislavsky. Divertingly beautiful, too, she went to Hollywood and enjoyed film success that made her, for a short time, the highest-paid actress in the country. But "Jazzy Nazzy" proved too independent for a male dominated industry and her star fell as quickly as it rose. Though frequently linked romantically to many men, including her "discovery" Valentino, and married twice, she was, at the very least, bisexual, and lived out her retired life with a female companion. And how's this for an odd twist? Was godmother to actress Nancy Davis (yes, Mrs. Nancy Reagan!). (*Author's collection*)

MOTION PICTURE
CLASSIC
DECEMBER   25¢

Nazimova   A BREWSTER PUBLICATION

luminary

top

C O L L E E N   M O O R E

K a t h l e e n   M o r r i s o n

Born August 19, 1900, in Port Huron, Michigan. Died 1988
Though fellow screen star Louise Brooks is often cited as the
advocate of the bobbed hair look that was so popular in the
1920s, it would be remiss not too mention that a demure
Moore was nearly as well regarded for her chopped top. A
favorite among moviegoers, Moore's short career crossed over
silents and talkies (though she hardly proved a formidable
presence in the latter). As a result of marrying twice to stock-
brokers and investing wisely, Moore retired early from films (in
the mid-'30s), managing to live most comfortably for the duration of her life. (*Kobal*)

bottom

C L A R A   B O W

Born August 25, 1905, in Brooklyn, New York. Died 1965
A woman who fully embodied the time in which she lived, Bow
was named the "It" girl (after the 1927 film) and as a result
became the feminine ideal of the Flapper age. We even have her
to thank for the cupid bow lip. However, despite the idolatry, it
didn't help that the scope of her fame lasted only a few years
(1927's Best Picture winner *Wings*, was one of the few true
highlights of her career). Her story is compelling and fraught
with scandal and mental illness. She attempted an ill-fated
comeback in 1933, and was not seen on celluloid since. For the
next thirty years, she seemingly never found happiness or a
repeat of her once bright existence. Clara ended her life living
in and out of sanitariums. (*MPTV*)

far right

G L O R I A   S W A N S O N

G l o r i a   J o s e p h i n e   M a e   S w e n s o n

Born March 27, 1897, in Chicago, Illinois. Died 1983
The epitome of early Hollywood glamour. Swanson came to
films with her then-husband (she married six times), actor Wallace Beery—the two met in Chicago. On their arrival at Key-
stone (Mack Sennett's studio), Swanson was cast in a series of
light comedies, at the behest of her hubby. In 1917, she
switched to Paramount and, under the auspices of Cecil B.
DeMille, became a star. But not just your "run-of-the-mill"
celebrity. For Swanson, stardom worked best with all the trappings—clothing, jewelry, houses, money, and men—and her public adored her glorious excess. She stayed a top actress into
talkies, Oscar-nominated twice during that period, for *Sadie
Thompson* (1928) and *The Trespasser* (1929). But, as it was for so
many silent stars, her time in the spotlight was over, or so it
seemed. In a most remarkable comeback, she played a faded
actress, Norma Desmond, in Wilder's *Sunset Boulevard* (1950). It
was a part, that for some, came uncannily close to real life—
Swanson's own. She was again Oscar-nominated, as was Bette
Davis (for *All About Eve*), but both lost to Judy Holliday (for *Born
Yesterday*); a good year for female parts. *Sunset*, however, did not
prove a career resuscitator, and Gloria appeared in only two
films shortly after, and a last film, *Airport 1975* (1974), playing
what else? a former movie star. (*Archive Photos*)

left

MARY TYLER MOORE

Born December 29, 1936, in Brooklyn, New York

After watching Mary Richards for seven years in "The Mary Tyler Moore Show" (1970–77), who would not want to emulate such an unperturbable heroine? (Or not want that first apartment?) Count me in, but it seems I stand at the end of a long line that formed back when she played Laura Petrie (on "The Dick Van Dyke Show," 1961–66). Starting simply as a dancer selling wares on television, Moore would go on to win eight Emmys (including special awards), a special Tony (for playing the "male" lead in *Whose Life Is It, Anyway?*), and an Oscar nomination for her portrayal of a cold-as-ice mother in *Ordinary People* (1980). She's even had time to write a bestselling autobiography, *After All.* (*Archive Photos*)

right

JANET GAYNOR

Laura Gainor

Born October 6, 1906, in Philadelphia, Pa. Died 1984

The first film actress to win an Academy Award, in 1928. Her statuette was given for not one, but three pictures, *Sunrise*, *Seventh Heaven* (both 1927) and *Street Angel* (1928). (By the early 1930s, the award would be given for one singular achievement.) Gaynor, an extremely likeable screen personality and a top box-office draw, smartly retired from movies at the top of her game. She married famed costume designer Adrian in 1939, and lived a great deal of the time in Brazil. She made one more theatrical film in 1957, *Bernadine*, and would only occasionally appear on television, including an episode of "The Love Boat." Her death, from pneumonia, was linked to injuries sustained in a car accident two years earlier, with actress Mary Martin. Her finest talking picture: the first *A Star Is Born* (1937). (*Author's collection*)

sweetheart

SHIRLEY TEMPLE

Born April 23, 1928, in Santa Monica, Ca. The most famous and popular child actress of all time. Though the sacrifice of her childhood for a world audience may have been worth the idolatry, it came at a price. Everything she did was watched, scrutinized, and copied by an adoring public—consisting mainly of mothers and children—but in her teen years stardom never came close to those early, starry heights. In fact, by the time she was twelve she was considered through with the business, despite the fact that she had grown into a fine-looking young lady, and one who could sing, dance, and act, too. What she could not accomplish (or recreate) after those heady, first years gave way to politics by her late thirties. A noted conservative, Temple lost her bid to an elected office, but was appointed to the U.N. by former President Nixon, and given ambassadorships to Ghana and Czechoslovakia. (*Paul Hesse/MPTV*)

JUNE ALLYSON
Eleanor Geisman
Born October 17, 1917, in the Bronx, New York
The quintessential "girl-next-door" with a husky voice and winning smile. A favorite MGM musical star in the '40s, playing the sweetheart, later more as the adoring wife in the '50s, and only rarely ever playing a baddie. Actor Dick Powell's wife from 1945 until his death in 1963. First film: *Best Foot Forward* (1943). Good typical role: *Good News* (1947). Best role against type: *The Shrike* (1955). (*Kobal*)

JEANNE CRAIN
Born May 25, 1925, in Barstow, California
A screen gem, Crain was a popular cinematic sweetheart who only occasionally broke out of saccharin roles to test the waters. Interestingly, when she did, she accomplished some of her best work: *A Letter to Three Wives* (1949) and *Pinky* (1950, and her Oscar nomination). By the 1950s, she became a glamorous mother of seven, but her career faltered (as so many others during the time did) by the early sixties. Once named "Camera Girl of 1942," she has not appeared on film since the mid-'70s. (*Tom Kelley/MPTV*)

E S T H E R   W I L L I A M S
Born August 8, 1923, in Los Angeles, California
Even though she was scouted by MGM as a swimmer, Williams' first few roles were light-hearted comedies—sans *l'eau*. Once the studio developed the capability to properly showcase their aquatic star, the Hollywood musical spectacular would never be the same. Through more than a dozen "splashy" films, she became an enormous worldwide success. Her special place in films will never be challenged. (*Archive Photos*)

S O N J A   H E N I E
Born April 8, 1910, in Oslo, Norway. Died 1969
A three-time Olympic gold medal winner (for figure skating), Henie was as unique a screen star as the aquatic Ms. Williams, though her films were not nearly as extravagant or well recalled. However, a cherubic Henie was for a time a top Fox star, who in kind made her ice-themed musicals little more than an excuse to see her skate. When her film career effectively ended in the late-1940s, Henie successfully took charge of (and appeared in) a nationwide traveling ice show. (*Author's collection*)

The main reason I learned to swim was because of Esther Williams (another was Mark Spitz, but that's another story). As a naive, starry-eyed youth, I was amazed that she could breathe underwater *and* come out of the pool looking so glamourous. How did she do it? I eventually uncovered the breathing mystery: tubes planted in the sea plants. But the glamour part? She was born that way!

Esther Williams on her career—
"I'd have to say unique. And they won't pick one ever again; the time has gone."

how it all started—
"During World War II, since there were no Olympic competitions, I was free to take part in activities that normal amateur athletic status wouldn't have allowed. I was appearing (in San Francisco) in Billy Rose's Aquacade (1940) and the people from MGM came to see me and the show. They were looking for someone to compete (theatrically) with Sonja Henie. As they said, they wanted to melt the ice and throw a swimmer in. I was the All-American girl—so I fit the bill."

reasons why it stopped—
"My movies were very difficult to make—it took a team of experts just to keep people from drowning. —No one wanted to see a middle-aged mermaid."

a unique "benefit" of her profession—
"Fred Astaire used to tell me how bothersome it could be when someone at a party would tell him how much they loved and admired his dancing and then expect him to dance right on the spot. I never had that problem; If an admirer told me how much they loved my work I was safe as long as they didn't fill up the room with water."

some thoughts about water—
"Water is magical; it's therapeutic, mentally and physically. Learning to swim helps you to overcome your fears. —Nothing has given me as much pleasure as working with blind children, teaching them to swim; they are exceptional. —A most wonderful compliment is when I hear from people that they learned to swim because of me."

a philosophic note—
"Don't look back—you may miss what happens tomorrow."

top

H O P E   L A N G E

Born November 28, 1931, in Redding Ridge, Connecticut
Sweetly sophisticated in 1959's *The Best of Everything* and sparring partner with none-other-than Joan Crawford, Hope debuted on the stage at age twelve. She became a two-time Emmy winner for her lead role in *The Ghost and Mrs. Muir* (based on the 1947 film classic) and Oscar-nominated for only her second screen appearance, *Peyton Place* (1957). Once married to actor Don Murray, then married-divorced-remarried to late director Alan J. Pakula. (*Everett*)

bottom

C O N N I E   S T E V E N S

Concetta Rosalie Ann Ingolia
Born August 8, 1938, in Brooklyn, New York
Cheerful nymph who was popular in films (*Rock-a-Bye, Baby*, 1958), television ("Hawaiian Eye"), and recordings ("Sixteen Reasons") from the late-'50s through the late-'60s, less so through the '70s and '80s. In recent years, via her still remarkably youthful appearance, Connie has been the purveyor of a successful line of cosmetics that bear her name. (*Corbis-Bettmann*)

far right

S A N D R A   D E E

Alexandra Zuck
Born April 23, 1942 in Bayonne, New Jersey
Cherubic child-model who debuted in films before she was fifteen. Once famously married to singer Bobby Darin, Dee had to endure becoming an icon of virginal youth, which never allowed her to mature gracefully in front of the cameras. Two back-to-back films from 1959, *Imitation of Life* and *A Summer Place* (also both massive hits) are possibly the best examples of her petite appeal. (*Corbis-Bettmann*)

I first became a fan of Shirley Jones when she starred in "The Partridge Family." I was just the right age to be one of her kids (in between Danny and Chris) and thought, how cool would it be to have a singing mom, my own musical group, *and* a customized yellow school bus. I "fell in love" when I saw her, finally, in *Oklahoma!, Carousel,* and especially as Marian the librarian in *The Music Man*—I was still too young to be watching *Elmer Gantry*. Here are some snippets from my heart-to-heart with "mom"—

Shirley Jones, on what she wanted to be—
"A veterinarian—I still love animals. I thought of my singing as secondary—a gift I took for granted. I figured I'd sing on the side."

what changed things—
"I was visiting a friend in New York and he suggested I sing for an agent he was acquainted with. He, in turn, sent me over to see (Richard) Rodgers and (Oscar) Hammerstein. I guess things went well, they cast me in the last six months that *South Pacific* played on Broadway. I was so young and naive—it all happened so easy."

the really big moment—
"To play the part of Laurie in the film version of *Oklahoma!* was a really big deal at the time. It seems they (Rodgers and Hammerstein) had me in mind for the role from the moment we first met."

the aftermath—
"Typecasting was much worse than today. After *April Love* I found myself out of work. In order to prove I could play more than the 'girl-next-door' I did dramatic television—and I even did a nightclub act (with then-husband Jack Cassidy) in Las Vegas."

her second coming—
"I appeared on Playhouse 90, and Burt Lancaster saw the show. At the time he was putting together the film *Elmer Gantry*. He told me he wanted me for the part of (the prostitute) Lulu Bains. It was the chance I was looking for. But director Richard Brooks had Piper Laurie in mind. Fortunately, for me, Burt won out. After viewing my first scene, Brooks came over and told me I was going to win the Oscar—and I did!"

why television—
"I was tired of traveling from place to place. I had a family and wanted to stay in California. They came to me with the idea for "The Partridge Family" (which was supposedly based on the real life performers, The Cowsills), without knowing they already had my stepson David in mind to appear with me. It was a wonderful, good time—I remember it with great fondness."

who she really is—
"I am the person you see. My feet are well-planted, and my thoughts are always with family, home, and hearth."

some words to live by—
"It's important to be who you are—you can't be liked by everybody. And enjoy every moment."

S H I R L E Y   J O N E S
Born March 31, 1934, in Smithton, Pennslyvania Though best known as the wholesome and lovely girl-next-door type (with a great singing voice, too) in such standout films as *Oklahoma!* (1955), *Carousel* (1956), and *The Music Man* (1962), and as one of TV-doms favorite moms (Shirley Partridge in "The Partridge Family"), Jones received her greatest praise by playing a prostitute in *Elmer Gantry* (1960). It also won her a best supporting actress Oscar. By her first husband, Jack Cassidy, she became stepmom to David and mother to Shaun. Of late, married to comedian/actor Marty Ingels and a recent-appointed chairman of the U.S. Leukemia Association. (*Corbis-Bettmann*)

left
ELIZABETH MONTGOMERY
Born April 15, 1933, in Los Angeles, California. Died 1994

Montgomery's show "Bewitched," beginning as a summer 1963 replacement and lasting for seven years, was destined from the start for TV immortality, just as one hoped would be the case for its delightful protagonist. None too ironically, this sitcom filled with beings who could de- and rematerialize at the twitch of a nose, saw the early demise of many of its enchanted cast, including Montgomery, Agnes Moorehead (Endora), Marion Lorne (Aunt Clara), and Alice Pearce (the first Mrs. Kravitz). Dispiriting, too, was the fact that Elizabeth was nominated five times for an Emmy, but never won. When the show ended, Liz went on to more (unrewarded) acclaim for two television-movies, *A Case of Rape* (1973) and *The Legend of Lizzie Borden* (1974). Incidentally, Elizabeth's father was acclaimed actor Robert Montgomery (who, himself, though nominated twice, did not win an Oscar). (*Everett*)

right, top
KAREN VALENTINE
Born 1948, in Sebastopol, California

Ingratiating comedic actress, who played the delightful young teacher Alice Johnson in the series "Room 222" (1969–74). It was a role that won her an Emmy. (*Ken Whitmore/MPTV*)

right, middle
SUSAN DEY
Born December 10, 1953, in Pekin, Illinois

A teen-boy favorite as Laurie in "The Partridge Family" (1970–74), a surprising dramatic actress in "Mary Jane Harper Cried Last Night" (1977), and holding her own in "LA Law" (1986–94), while picking up three Emmy nominations (1986, '87, and '88). (*Everett*)

right, bottom
SALLY FIELD
Born November 6, 1946, in Pasadena, California

We first laid eyes on this adorable cherub when she became television's "Gidget," then most amusingly as "The Flying Nun" (a role that for years was hard for her to play down). However, after much persevering, she was cast in the telefilm *Sybil* (1977) and won the Emmy; it changed the course of her career. She went on to much theatrical film acclaim, including two Oscar-winning Best Actress turns for *Norma Rae* (1979) and *Places in the Heart* (1984). However, it may be for the latter's acceptance speech that she will be forever remembered. (*Curt Gunther/MPTV*)

following spread
BROOKE SHIELDS
Born May 1, 1965, in New York City, NY

A beauty, inside and out, from her start as a child model to her recent popular sitcom "Suddenly Susan." (*Andrew Eccles*)

some not so random thoughts from our Miss Brooke—

"Having been in the business for so long I've never known anonymity, so I don't really know what I was missing. • From the very beginning there was something about it that I liked; I think it was in direct proportion to getting approval. • I have had a lot of fun and have no regrets. The negative criticism has not stopped me, I take it all with a grain of salt. • Everyone can't love you; try enjoying your time with the seventy-five percent of the room that cares about you instead of going after the twenty-five percent that doesn't. • I'm a sucker for "pretty" just like most people, but I've learned how quickly it goes away when you don't like the person. • Looking at what I've done, I still try to do better. I can see the difference when I feel confident—it shows through."

left

NATALIE WOOD
Natasha Gurdin
Born July 20, 1938, in San Francisco, Ca. Died 1981
Wood first came to our attention as a child star, most fondly in *Miracle on 34th Street* (1947). As she grew older, her preadolescent cuteness gave way to unabashed teenage prettiness, as witnessed in *Rebel Without a Cause* (1955), which also held promise for her as an actress of note, with a first Oscar nomination (as best supporting actress). With the 1950s drawing to a close, Wood matured into one of the most appealing beauties on film and a delight in the screen (melo)dramatization of Herman Wouk's *Marjorie Morningstar* (1958). By the 1960s, Wood was a worldclass stunner, her beauty a seamless blend of youthful innocence and womanly sensuality. This was her decade, and she made the most of it. Surprisingly, for all her charms, she was not a critic's favorite, even though two more films garnered her Oscar nominations, *Splendor in the Grass* (1961) and *Love with the Proper Stranger* (1963). After her remarriage to actor Robert Wagner in 1972, she would appear in very few films. Her last, *Brainstorm* (1983), was still being filmed when she died in a boating accident. (*Archive Photos*)

right

LUISE RAINER
Born January 10, 1910, in Vienna, Austria
A remarkable talent and a remarkable career, given its huge success and rapid end. Hauntingly lovely Luise became the first two-time and back-to-back Oscar-winner (as Best Actress) in films, for *The Great Ziegfeld*, 1936, and *The Good Earth*, 1937. In them, she maximized her evocative acting style to great effect, creating memorable roles out of two haunting heroines, Anna Held and O-Lan. Just as startling, her subsequent films were disastrous. Blame for these career miscalculations have been leveled at studio head Louis B. Mayer, her then-husband, playwright Clifford Odets, and Luise herself, who was said to be somewhat exacting. Her last film was made in 1943; in total, only twelve. (*Author's collection*)

flora & fauna

The phone is ringing somewhere in Paris, I imagine the sound bouncing off ornately papered walls—something very Beatonesque. A machine picks up, and I hear a faintly familiar female voice, first in French, then switching to English. Oh my God, it's her! I have Leslie Caron's answering machine! But how oddly disquieting it was knowing she had one (and a fax, too)—I so associate her with another time and place. Not of the past, though, but somewhere quite romantic. And let's face it, neither of these two contraptions could be considered the least bit romantic. I leave my message—nothing I say seems to come out right—and hang up. The next morning, I try again. Something tells me I better be prepared. My instincts are correct—after three rings the phone is answered, this time by a real person. Voila! it is her—I am talking with Leslie Caron—wait 'til I tell mom!

Of few actresses can it be said that they "sparkle," which is different from "shine" or "glitter" (however, it is close to "twinkle"—and both involve, I believe, pixie dust). Caron is one of these special women. Through her entire career, beginning to now, in every performance, she has a light that dances all around you, even if you're just sitting in the audience. For someone so dazzling to the eye, I was curious what her first impressions were of Tinseltown (back in its "golden age"). She told me, "Hollywood seemed very calm—unlike what I imagined. It was a place where people would go to bed at 9:oo in the evening and get up at 6:oo the next morning. I was disappointed—I missed the glamour of Paris." But what brought her to films was itself quite a glamourous story: Since she was sixteen, Caron danced in the ballet. As a member of Roland Petit's famed troupe she would tour all over Europe, and was praised throughout the continent. One evening in Paris, Gene Kelly was attending an opening night performance of *La Rencontre* in which Caron danced the lead and was so taken by her (as so many have been before or since) that he kept her in mind when looking for a partner for his upcoming film, *An American in Paris*. When the time came, he asked her to do a screen test—but *without* his studio's consent. He needn't have worried—his instincts were right on the mark—within a few weeks she was off to California, cast as the female lead. It goes on to win the Oscar for Best Picture of 1951, and makes Caron a star.

Lili (1953) appears a short while later. It is a hard picture to describe without it sounding childish. That's because Caron spends much of her time onscreen with a quartet of puppets. (Asked if it was difficult playing opposite four wooden friends, Ms. Caron charmingly notes, "When you talk to puppets long enough, they do begin to seem real.") So don't let preconceived notions dissuade you, the film has quite a bit to say, to children *and* adults, plus a great deal of heart, something many "modern" pictures lack completely. In fact, the honesty of the work was so convincing it earned Caron her first Oscar nomination and the film one for Best Picture. What is most surprising was the lack of initial support the film recieved from MGM. It was a "modest" movie and considered a step down for such a glamourous new star—many around the studio bemoaned her sad circumstances. But Caron had the right instinct, she knew she couldn't go wrong if she listened to her own heart.

From her rollicking, frolicking *Gigi* (Best Picture, 1958), to the marvelous dramatic role in *The L-Shaped Room* (1963, and a second Oscar nom), up to her recent work in *Damage* (1992), Caron remains a charming, enchanting figure. But she tells me she has always felt uncomfortable with fame—she says that it used to terrify her just being in a room with more than two people. (Of the many things she learned from films was how to speak and appear in front of large groups of people.) But innate shyness is only one part of her allure, the rest is a big part French, a smidgen of dance, dramatic forte when needed, a cheshire-cat grin, and that all-important sprinkle of magic powder—pixie dust.

LESLIE CARON
Born July 1, 1931, in Boulogne-Billancourt, Fr. First film: *An American in Paris* (seven Oscars, including Best Picture, 1951). Two-time Oscar-nominee, for *Lili* (1953) and *The L-shaped Room* (1963). Also starred in *Gigi* (eight Oscars, including Best Picture, 1958). (*Archive Photos*)

left, top
ANGELA BASSETT
Born August 16, 1958, in New York City, NY
An Oscar nomination (playing Tina Turner) in *What's Love Got To Do With It?* (1993) may have placed Bassett on the map, but sooner or later one would have assuredly taken notice of this dynamic and devastatingly beautiful actress. Films following *Love*, with the exception of the divine *Waiting to Exhale* (1995), have not taken proper advantage of this powerhouse performer. But for Angela, more of those mesmerizing moments are no doubt in the works. (*Robert Trachtenberg/Corbis-Outline*)

left, bottom
TAINA ELG
Born March 9, 1930, in Helsinki, Finland
Though she would appear in only a few films, Elg was an entrancing, elegant gamine. As a dancer she shown brightly, if all too briefly, in the delectable Cole Porter musical *Les Girls* (1957). Made an appearance in the 1991 film *Leibestraum*. (*Corbis-Bettmann*)

right
JEAN SEBERG
Born November 13, 1938, in Marshalltown, Iowa. Died 1979
Seberg's first outing was as the title heroine in Otto Preminger's *Saint Joan* (1957). Despite the extraordinary publicity build-up, via a worldwide talent search, the finished film was a disaster. Fortunately, subsequent roles in European films proved better vehicles for her subtle and seductive charms. Two particular performances, in *Breathless* (1960) and *Lilith* (1964), are considered seminal. However, disaster continued to loom, both professionally and personally, with unmitigated mistakes, such as the musical *Paint Your Wagon* (1969). Also, her close relationship with the political organization The Black Panthers was treated with great hostility from all factions. She was married four times, but officially only three. Unstable mental health may have been instrumental in her death from a drug overdose; it was ruled a probable suicide. (*Corbis-Bettmann*)

left

A U D R E Y   H E P B U R N
Born May 4, 1929, near Brussels, Belgium. Died 1993
Hepburn had the four elements necessary to
become a cinematic icon—style, talent, beauty, and
originality—making her one of film's most beloved
actresses. Add to that her charity, and she became
one of the most beloved women ever. The winner
of a Best Actress Oscar (for *Roman Holiday*, in
1953) and Tony (for *Ondine*, that same year), she
was "discovered" by authoress Colette, and cast
to play the female lead in her nonmusical version
of *Gigi* (1951). Though she would be Oscar-nominated four times more, her acting always took second place to her reedy and fragile, couture-laden
loveliness, which was luminous. Amusingly, she is
probably one of the most memorable criers on
film; look and listen to her emotional jags in *Breakfast at Tiffany's* (1962) and *Wait Until Dark* (1967).
She is sorely missed. (*Archive Photos*)

right

M I A   F A R R O W
Maria De Lourdes Villiers Farrow
Born February 9, 1945, in Los Angeles, California
Born the daughter of a director (John Farrow)
and an actress (Maureen O'Sullivan) it seemed
preordained that she become an actress, too, but
it was her offscreen entanglements that drew Mia
the most attention. When she was appearing in
the television version of "Peyton Place" she drew
the interest of Frank Sinatra. Though he was thirty years older than she, they were married in
1966. They divorced two years later. Farrow even
made headlines when she cut her hair (with the
help of master stylist Vidal Sassoon). Her role as
the mother in Roman Polanski's *Rosemary's Baby*
(1968) drew raves from critics and audiences, but
her ascent into superstardom was interrupted by
her relationship (and subsequent marriage) to
conductor Andre Previn. However, it would be
her collaboration, both professional and personal,
with Woody Allen over the course of a decade
that spawned the most discussion. And most of
us know how that coupling ended. Little seen in
films today, Farrow devotes most of her time and
attention to her houseful of children, both adopt-
ed and natural born. (*Archive Photos*)

WINONA RYDER

Winona Laura Horowitz
Born October, 1971, in Winona, Minnesota
Named for her hometown, Winona moved to San Francisco at age four and took up acting at age eleven. Debuting in films when she was fifteen, Ryder quickly established herself as a talented neo-ingenue type, more complex than your average teenager, and quickly rose above the pack. Role after role has reinforced early praise, picking up two Oscar nominations along the way (for *The Age of Innocence*, 1993, and *Little Women*, 1994). (*Matthew Jordan Smith/Corbis-Outline*)

JULIA ROBERTS

Born October 28, 1967, in Smyrna, Georgia
The rarest of commodities—a female actress whose films open big at the box office. No surprise, then, that she has become the industry's highest paid woman with a current asking price of $20 million a picture. Such actions are not generated by single, substantive weekends alone, as the "legs" of her films can attest—*Pretty Woman* (1990), *Pelican Brief* (1993), *My Best Friend's Wedding* (1997). More than just a pretty face (with a grin from ear to ear), Roberts has two Oscar nominations to her credit (for *Steel Magnolias*, 1988, and *Pretty Woman*) and with the likelihood of that number rising to be a very safe bet. Younger sister of actor Eric Roberts. (*Albert Sanchez/Corbis-Outline*)

CHER

Cherilyn LaPiere Sarkisian
Born May 20, 1946, in El Centro, California
An unstoppable force. Almost no one has had the staying power, or talent, to remain at the top of her game like Cher. Beginning with her first hit single with Sonny, "I Got You Babe" (1965), to her biggest smash ever, "Believe" (1998), pop music is only one of the places where she rules unchallenged; she has conquered television, theater, and movies, too. Not bad for a woman who had an inconstant childhood (her mother was married ten times) and is as often criticized for her free-spirited lifestyle (which is what we love about her) and fabulous wardrobe, as she is praised for her contributions to entertainment (which are infinite). An Oscar winner for *Moonstruck* (1987). Is there anything she can't do?

S U Z Y   P A R K E R
Born October 28, 1933, in San Antonio, Texas

When the worlds of fashion and film overlap. Though someone who could be an exceptional beauty in any decade, Parker was fifties glamour personified. Her attempt to be a film star was not surprising. Others, like Lauren Bacall, had met with great success. And no doubt Parker had hoped she could bring some of that willowy couture elegance and sophistication to film. Unfortunately, she was met with little success, and her bright hopes soon faded. Nevertheless, for her few all-too-brief moments on the screen she was a devastating sight. Take a look at *The Best of Everything* (1959). (*Archive Photos*)

mannequin

MADELEINE CARROLL
Born Feb. 26, 1906, in West Bromwich, Eng. Died 1987
An early Hitchcock blond, especially noteworthy in his British-made classic *The 39 Steps* (1935). When this sleek beauty found her way to Hollywood a short time later, she was met with equal success in films as diverse as *The Prisoner of Zenda* (1937) and *My Favorite Blonde* (1942). She retired from films in 1949. (*Kobal*)

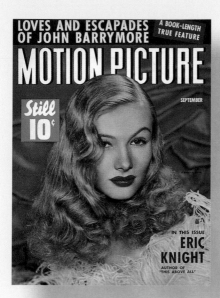

right

V E R O N I C A   L A K E

Constance Frances Marie Ockelman

Born November 14, 1919, in Brooklyn, NY. Died 1973

Lake had a tumultuous life that ended, with her death by hepatitis, in near-obscurity. During the mid-1940s, however, her popularity was unquestioned. Even her "peek-a-boo" hairstyle was so widely copied that the government asked that she wear it another way, at least through the end of the war; it seems women who sported the long tresses were getting them caught in factory machines. A most memorable film: *I Married a Witch* (1942). Her best screen pairing: with Alan Ladd in *This Gun For Hire* (1942). (*Author's collection*)

blondie

left
LAUREN BACALL
Betty Joan Perske
Born September 16, 1924 in the Bronx, New York
A cat-like Bacall was quickly dubbed "the Look" by her studio Warner Bros. and vaulted to stardom with her screen debut in *To Have to Have Not* (1945) opposite her soon-to-be husband, Humphrey Bogart. With a sultry stare that could send your blood racing, Bacall, a one-time model who began acting on the stage, did not get the type of critical praise for her fewer-than-expected acting turns as one might expect from such a legendary career—that is until a final Oscar nom, in 1996, for *The Mirror Has Two Faces*. Once married to actor Jason Robards, Jr., Lauren has received two Tonys for Broadway triumphs in *Applause* (1970), a musical retelling of *All About Eve*, and *Woman of the Year*, ten years later. (*MPTV*)

right
JOAN FONTAINE
Joan De Beauvoir de Havilland
Born October 22, 1917, in Tokyo, Japan
Cool and calculating beauty, whose career took off, after a few years of stumbling, by playing shy, downcast types, most effectively in *Rebecca* (Best Picture, 1940, and her first AAN) and *Suspicion* (1941, her Oscar winner). A third-time nominee for *The Constant Nymph* (1943), Fontaine is also an accomplished outdoorswoman, interior decorator, chef, pilot, balloonist, and author. Sister of Olivia DeHavilland, though they are far from being on sisterly terms. (*Kobal*)

As a little boy growing up in the Midwest, I was always fascinated with movies (and movie stars). Typically, you would find me cross-legged on the hardwood floor in front of our black-and-white Zenith, tuned to the broadcast of some amusing (often mind-numbing) confection. The local syndicated stations offered me fare like the "early" matinee, a "five-star" movie, creature features, and the late, late show. I was not selective—I tried to watch them all. In this pastime I was not alone; my mother carried with her an enormous appreciation for motion pictures when she moved from Korea after she had married my father, and this special fondness worked its way through me. For the two of us they represented an escape. Of course, as a kid I had little to be running from, but the same could not be said of my mother. Coming from a small, war-torn country, seeing any Hollywood-made, Technicolor, star-studded production *was* an escape. Films represented to her what the world could be like. She believed the fantasy and, in turn, so did I. As would be expected, she also developed a deep devotion to the talent in those films. There was a long list of favorites: for the men it was Montgomery Clift, Charlton Heston, William Holden, and more. For the ladies, the group included Ava Gardner, Elizabeth Taylor, Audrey Hepburn, and so on. But over the years I tend to recall one name, which stands out from the rest—Kim Novak. Whenever she appeared on the screen, you could count on my mother proffering, unsolicited, how Novak was "number one" or "top." If she offered anything else I usually didn't bother paying much attention, so enrapt was I with the vision before me. Her image formed a template in my head, which has stayed with me ever since.

When we spoke, she told me of how I "touched her shoulder," as a way of reminding her my book was nearing deadline. She was painting while we talked, somewhere on her ranch in Oregon. How wonderful it was to be able to think of her beside a canvas, while the wind softly blew through her hair—of course I was fantasizing, imagining her outside by the ocean, like a scene from *Vertigo*. I had many questions to ask, but none seemed relevant. What would she tell me that others (myself included) didn't already know? I soon realized it was not what she would say, but how. Here was a woman who had endured so much, good and bad, that melancholy and resolve was infused in her every response. She told me, "I had a destiny—I knew I would be a communicator—but I was the shyest child. I hadn't planned on being an actress; but by not preparing for it I felt more honest. As an actress, you mimic—I tried not to be someone else—I wanted to be myself." And she was. Of the top female stars of her time, it could be said that Novak was one of the most enigmatic, a unique and smooth blending of the cool with the hot—making her unforgettable *and* irresistible. But being so universally worshipped had its shortcomings, she told me: "Fame was difficult, I had not planned on sharing my life that way. Some enjoyed it—for me it wasn't easy. Maybe if I *had* prepared to be an actress I wouldn't have been as affected. But it was a Catch-22—I adored what it had to offer, it allowed me to share with others. But it did make me very self-conscious—the interest in my lifestyle, the press, the expectations."

The business Novak said goodbye to years ago is today a different animal—still a mystical beast, but not imbued with the same powers. Now a star is more or less left to her own devices—no longer protected by a single studio's personnel but also not domineered by a single studio head or manipulated by a single studio's vision. "The industry likes to put you in a box. It became difficult to express myself. But you need your own identity—I was aware of not wanting *it* to be lost" she laments. Being a star today, then, might be better for her. In agreement, she says, "It's far more the period for me now. I could be much more of myself, less of the studio." It's intriguing to think of what type of star she would become had she stumbled into films in 1999, not 1954. However, she is not completely solicitous in her view of current film fare, saying, "[Films] are more shocking, more violent and more sexual than they need to be. A film should try to stimulate the interest and stir the imagination of the viewer, but not answer *all* the questions."

But at least one of mine was answered. Even though the pure fantasy attraction to films has long since left me, when I spoke with Kim Novak I found out how human our "stars" can be. So my question was answered. Momentarily, I brought the pure fantasy back; when I conjured up the vision of my dream movie of course Kim Novak was there, looking sumptuous in a black, backless Jean Louis gown. Only this time beneath that satin-swathed facade lurked a woman I knew firsthand had feelings just like mine, loved her work—painting, writing *and* her films—and tried to follow her own path in life.

KIM NOVAK
Marilyn Pauline Novak
Born February 13, 1933, in Chicago, Illinois
Combining both ladylike aloofness *and* sensuality, Novak was as big a star as they come. Discovered and groomed by Columbia head Harry Cohn, Kim came up from the ranks to take her place alongside Taylor, Gardner, and Monroe as the reigning goddesses of the fifties. A number of her films are highly regarded, from *Picnic* to *Vertigo*, *Pal Joey* to *Bell, Book and Candle*. But like Monroe, Novak was never given her due when it came to acting praise. (The closest she may have come was a Most Promising Newcomer Golden Globe in 1954.) Though she obviously fulfilled that promise, by the late-'60s she had had enough of Hollywood. Nowadays, she paints, writes, and actively pursues the care of animals, only occasionally appearing before the public on very special occasions, such as the rerelease of *Vertigo* in 1998, when she looked and sounded as ravishing as ever. (*Corbis-Bettmann*)

Janet Leigh was a senior in college studying music and psychology and had never given acting much thought. That is, until a chance encounter with legendary star Norma Shearer, whom she met while both were on a skiing holiday. Keeping an eye out for new talent, the ever-alert Shearer knew she had something in the fresh-faced Leigh. She notified her friend producer Lew Wasserman, of her discovery. At the time, he was looking for just such a girl to play opposite Van Johnson (in *The Romance of Rosy Ridge*, 1947). Leigh was signed, and the picture — a hit. By the time she married actor Tony Curtis a few years later, Leigh was a star, and the twosome became one of America's favorite couples.

But their fairy tale existence was not without its problems. Being such a photogenic duo made them constant subjects of the popular media (sound familiar?), prompting Leigh to take matters into her own hands. She said, "It became necessary to set up rules and boundaries. As far as I was concerned, when I left my house I belonged to the public, but in my house you were not welcome unless invited." However, she cautions that a balance must be kept when dealing with the rewards of fame, "We are who we are because of the audience. Their interest in us should be appreciated. We have a responsibility to them that goes with the territory." Offered as some final words on the subject, Leigh comments, "Try to give both the fan and yourself some dignity."

At a moment when movies were fast losing ground to television (the late-1950s to early-'60s), three of Leigh's films proved that what was possible to do on the big screen could not (yet) be as successfully duplicated on the small. Even for movies, this cinematic triple — *Touch of Evil, Pyscho, Manchurian Candidate* — was unusual. Each, in their own way, stretched the limits of film subject matter and presentation. Of her part, Leigh is most modest, "When directors like (Orson) Welles and (Alfred) Hitchcock approach you to do a film, you know it will be special and different. But ultimately, the audience decides if it will be accepted and what the lasting effect is." (Incidentally, Leigh was nominated for a Best Supporting Actress Oscar for *Pyscho*, 1960.)

Knowing that we have come very far from the "shower" scene in Psycho, Leigh doesn't hesitate in her praise of today's advances in film technology but, not surprisingly, is less enthusiastic about the quality of the stories that form their core. "We don't seem to reach as high," but she adds, "It's a business, if people didn't go to see these films, they wouldn't make them." Of that you can be sure.

left
J A N E T   L E I G H
Jeanette Helen Morrison
Born July 6, 1927, in Merced, California
(*Corbis-Bettmann*)

right
E V A   M A R I E   S A I N T
Born July 4, 1924, in Newark, New Jersey
This serene, youthful beauty has appeared in far too few films. But among them can be counted at least two genuine cinema classics, *On the Waterfront*, 1954, and *North by Northwest*, 1958. In the former, her film debut, she won the Best Supporting Actress Oscar, and in the latter, shone seductively as a beguiling Hitchcock-blond spy. (*Corbis-Bettmann*)

near right
TIPPI HEDREN

Nathalie Kay Hedren

Born January 19, 1931, in Lafayette, Minnesota

A sleek model who was made a star by Alfred Hitchcock as the female lead in two of his films, *The Birds* (1963) and *Marnie* (1964). She was perfectly cast as his icy-blond protagonist but seemed to suffer in films without his guidance. In recent years, this mother of actress Melanie Griffith has become an advocate of animal welfare, particularly big cats. Grrrr. (*Corbis-Bettmann*)

far right
FAYE DUNAWAY

Born January 14, 1941, in Bascom, Florida

A slick, "fashion-plate" actress of marked determinedness, who took the moviegoing world by storm with her icy heroine, Bonnie Parker, in *Bonnie and Clyde* (1967, and her first AAN). She was an enormous star for the next decade, through her Oscar win for *Network* (1976), slipping a bit in stature by the eighties. Her screen crescendos have been sorely missed since last put to great effect in *Mommie Dearest* (1981). Recent roles tend to soften the blows of her forceful, dynamic personality. (*David Sutton/MPTV*)

PHOTOPLAY

SEPTEMBER   25 CENTS

ANN
HARDING
BY
TCHETCHET

Is HEPBURN Killing Her Own CAREER?

left
A N N   H A R D I N G
Dorothy Walton Gatley
Born Aug. 7, 1901, in Fort Sam Houston, Tex. Died 1981
Harding was a major star for just a brief
period of time and specialized in playing
poised and civilized leading ladies, typically
in tearjerkers, and was Oscar-nominated
once, for *Holiday* (1930). She retired from
films in 1937 but returned a number of
years later, often cast as a refined matri-
arch. (*Author's collection*)

right
M E R L E   O B E R O N
Estelle Merle O'Brien Thompson
Born February 19, 1911, in Bombay, India. Died 1979
Of Ceylonese and British parentage, a
scintillatingly lovely Oberon became a
star upon being discovered by legendary
producer Alexander Korda. Not a particularly gifted actress, Merle (who did manage an Oscar nomination for *Dark Angel*,
1935) had a special beauty that made her
screen appearances transcendent. However, roles in a number of classic films,
including *Wuthering Heights* (1939) and *A
Song to Remember* (1945) are made just as
remarkable by her able handling of the
lead female parts. After appearing inter-
mittently in films until the late-'50s, a
four-times married Merle (last to Robert
Wolders in 1973) lived out the entirety
of her life in resplendence, befitting one
so regal. (*Kobal*)

lady

far left

JANE WYMAN

Sarah Jane Fulks
Born January 4, 1914, in St. Joseph, Missouri

Likely, Wyman will be most remembered for being the first wife of Ronald Reagan (from 1940 to 1948) or as the villainous Angela Channing in television's "Falcon Crest." Yet, her entire list of credits is far more impressive. A four-time Oscar nominee, with a win for *Johnny Belinda* (1948), Wyman started out as a light singer (on radio) before turning her attentions to Hollywood. As a comedic blonde, she enjoyed marginal success. However, her role in *The Lost Weekend* (Best Picture, 1944) changed the direction of her career. On the strength of this performance she was given ever more demanding roles. From family fare, *The Yearling* (1946), to "weepies" like *The Magnificent Obsession* (1954), and frothy comedies, *Here Comes the Groom* (1951), Wyman proves herself a most diverse talent. (*Photofest*)

top

LORETTA YOUNG

Gretchen Michaela Young
Born January 6, 1913, in Salt Lake City Utah

A glowing screen (and television) presence. Young began as an extra, left for convent school (undoubtedly influencing her later performances in *The Bishop's Wife* [1947] and *Come Back to the Stable* [1949]), then went back into films in 1927. Easily crossing into sound films, she was a major star throughout the 1930s and '40s, peaking with her Oscar-winner, *The Farmer's Daughter* (1947). By her early forties, Young switched to the small screen, and was a very popular household presence for eight years. The self-titled show brought her three Emmys but is renowned for her showstopping entrances, with Young decked out in a most beautiful and everchanging wardrobe. (*Kobal*)

middle

GREER GARSON

Born September 29, 1908, in County Down, Ireland. Died 1996

Personifying the "lady," Garson had no peers. Appearing in just over a dozen theatrical films, she was Oscar-nominated seven times. Remarkable under most circumstances (she won for 1943's *Mrs. Miniver*), Greer's career rushed into high gear (at MGM) to fill the void being created by departing Greta Garbo and Norma Shearer (who turned down the role in *Miniver*). As beloved as she was, Garson's love affair with audiences declined by the late-'40s. Fortunately, she married well and left films, returning sporadically to act (in theater and movies), and, on occasion, lending her magnificent voice to narration. (*Kobal*)

bottom

NORMA SHEARER

Born August 10, 1900, in Montreal, Canada. Died 1983

The familiar adage goes, "It's not what you know, but whom." Certainly, in Hollywood, knowing the right person can get you very far. Many have argued that Shearer owes her stardom to marriage with MGM wunderkind, producer Irving G. Thalberg. Certainly his guidance helped to direct her talent into the right roles; without him (he died in 1936) she turned down leads in *Gone With the Wind* and *Mrs. Miniver* (the latter, for instance, because she felt her fans could not accept seeing her as the mother of an adult child.) However, during her rule as queen of the lot, Shearer was Oscar-nominated six times, including *The Barretts of Wimpole Street* (1934), *Romeo and Juliet* (1936), a role for which she was far too old, and *Marie Antoinette* (1938), winning for 1930's *The Divorcee*. She is also a memorable member of the campy delight *The Women* (1939). Shearer retired from films in 1942. (*Kobal*)

left

DEBORAH KERR

Born Sept. 30, 1921, in Helensburgh, Scotland

A gifted, enigmatic screen presence. Any film with Kerr appearing in it is worth watching. Her serenity, even under the most profane or boisterous circumstances, is inescapable; you cheer her even when she's playing the wanton (*From Here to Eternity*, Best Picture 1953). From her humble English film beginning to her retirement in 1969, she was nominated for six Oscars (including ...*Eternity*, 1953; *The King and I*, 1956; and *Separate Tables*, 1958) but never took home the golden statuette. This was "corrected" with an honorary award in 1997. Her 1947 classic, *Black Narcissus*, is breathtaking. (*Corbis-Bettmann*)

right

GRACE KELLY

Born Nov. 12, 1928, in Phila., Pa. D. 1982

An American fairy tale with an all-too-human end. Kelly was born into wealth and prosperity in the "Mainliner" area of northern Philly and had always aspired to be an actress. Interestingly, her first forays into the spotlight were met with indifference. Eventually, a Broadway part would lead to one in Hollywood; by her second film she would play Gary Cooper's wife in the western classic *High Noon* (1952). An Oscar nomination for *Mogambo*, the following year, was succeeded in 1954 with a year of superstardom—*Rear Window*, *Dial M for Murder*, and her Oscar turn in *The Country Girl*. Her third in a trio of films for Alfred Hitchcock (*To Catch a Thief*, 1955) took her to Monaco for location scenes. It was there that she met Prince Rainier, romance ensued, and the two would soon be wed. Upon the ceremony in 1956, she retired from films (making only eleven in total) and became a citizen of the world. It was always rumored that she was interested in making a return to movies, although the right project never worked itself out. Tragically, the opportunity to do so would end with her death. Suffering from an attack, she lost control of her car, and it careened off a mountain road. (*Archive Photos*)

I R E N E   D U N N E

Born December 20, 1898, in Louisville, Kentucky. Died 1990
Prettily prim and proper Irene began her career as an accomplished singer, most memorably (as Magnolia) in the original production of *Showboat* (1937). A five-time Oscar nominee, this devout Republican made a profession out of playing upright, slightly moralistic, but always lovable female denizens of oft-times wacky environs. A broad swath of worthy films, including *Cimarron* (Best Picture, 1931, and her first AAN), *The Awful Truth* (1937, AAN), *Anna and the King of Siam* (1946), and *I Remember Mama* (1948, AAN) marks her illustrious sojourn in Hollywood. (*Glenn Embree/MPTV*)

bottom

J E N N I F E R   J O N E S
P h y l l i s   I s l e y
Born March 2, 1919, in Tulsa, Oklahoma
A quite-capable actress, who, in the right hands, became a major Hollywood player. Jones had an angelic beauty, seen to its best advantage in her Oscar-winner *Song of Bernadette* (1944). This film was the first in a series carefully selected by then-husband producer David O. Selznick. (She was previously married to actor Robert Walker; the union did not end on good terms.) Over the next two decades, she tested the limits of her acting ability, often with great results—*Madame Bovary* (1949), *Carrie* (1952), and *Love is a Many Splendored Thing* (1955). Widowed from Selznick in 1965, she married industrialist Norton Simon in 1971. (*Archive Photos*)

right

C E L E S T E   H O L M
Born April 29, 1919, in New York City
Broadway's original Ado Annie, in *Oklahoma!* Oscar-nominated three times, for *Gentlemen's Agreement* (1947, her winner), *Come to the Stable* (1949), and *All About Eve* (1950). Played the best fairy godmother, ever, in the 1966 telebroadcast of "Rodgers and Hammerstein's Cinderella." (*Glenn Embree/MPTV*)

If any actress could be considered a role model, look no further than Celeste Holm. Her films (and film roles) had something to say, and she conveyed those messages with a most engaging personality.

Celeste Holm on her appeal—
"People think they can trust me (and they can). If I say I'll do it, I will."

her inspirations—
"I saw Pavlova dance when I was 2 1/2 years old. She gave herself to the audience. I felt what a gift it was to be human. I wanted to give the audience that present. • My grandmother (an editor) and mother (an artist), together, combined discipline with creativity."

the profession—
"As an actor, strength lies in allowing yourself to depend on the other players. • You can never give enjoyment to an audience unless you are enjoying what you are doing."

on today's films—
"Most of them are rubbish. They have nothing much to say and the people who make them seem to have no sense of responsibility."

movie MIRROR

AUGUST

10¢

A MACFADDEN PUBLICATION

JEAN ARTHUR

HOW HOLLYWOOD TRIED TO SPOIL THE
Jeanette MacDonald—Gene Raymond Marriage
IS ROBERT TAYLOR'S MOTHER HAPPY?

left
JEAN ARTHUR
Gladys Georgianna Greene
Born October 17, 1905, in New York City, NY. Died 1991
Arthur was a unique, engaging talent
who excelled in comedies of the late-
1930s and early-'40s. Some of her best
work was for director Frank Capra, who
called her his favorite actress. She was
Oscar-nominated for the wartime comedy *The More the Merrier* (1943), but
appeared afterward in only four more
films, including her last movie *Shane*
(1953). (*Author's collection*)

right
CAROLE LOMBARD
Jane Alice Peters
Born October 6, 1908, in Fort Wayne, Indiana. Died 1942
At the time of her tragic death, by plane
crash, Lombard was one of the screen's
most-beloved stars—not only to audiences, but especially to her adoring husband, Clark Gable. President Roosevelt
sent a grieving Gable condolences on
behalf of himself and the entire nation—
the ill-fated flight was part of a war-bond
selling tour. A most able and witty come-
dienne, Lombard languished for years as a
contract player until her breakthrough in
Twentieth Century (1934). The "screwball"
comedy became her staple, through such
rib-ticklers as *My Man Godfrey* (1936) and
Nothing Sacred (1937). Also once married
to actor William Powell. (*Photofest*)

funny girl

left

LUCILLE BALL

Born August 6, 1911, outside of Jamestown, NY. Died 1989

This most beloved of comics began as a Goldwyn Girl, though many of her pre-television film appearances were less than memorable, including the infrequent dramatic parts. However, her meeting with Cuban band leader Desi Arnaz, on the RKO set in 1940, would lead to one of the most popular (and important) couplings in show business. Married in 1941, Lucy and Desi hit paydirt with the television debut of "I Love Lucy." Regarded as one of the most influential shows of all time, it lasted, surprisingly, for only six seasons before being replaced by a bastardized version, entitled "The Lucy-Desi Comedy Hour." The show's popularity, along with that of its production company, Desilu, made Ball a formidable Hollywood presence. Through "The Lucy Show," "Here's Lucy," and "Life with Lucy," Ball continued to act only sporadically in other mediums, including *Wildcat* (1960) on Broadway, and films, such as *Yours, Mine and Ours* (1968). Over her two decades as a queen of television comedy, Lucy would place four Emmys on her mantelpiece. (*Photofest*)

right

PAULA PRENTISS

Paula Ragusa

Born on March 4, 1939, in San Antonio, Texas

Gifted comedic and dramatic actress, with a lovable drawl and lanky, good looks. Film debut, as the forlorn co-ed in *Where the Boys Are* (1960). Other credits include *Man's Favorite Sport?*, *The World of Henry Orient* (both 1964) and as the best friend turned robotron in *The Stepford Wives* (1975). Even her briefest appearances (*The Parallax View*, 1974) kept you wanting more. Emmy-nominee for her (and husband's) television show "He & She" (1968). (*Corbis-Bettmann*)

There wasn't anybody I wanted to speak with more than Paula Prentiss. From the first moment I saw her I was hooked; She looked so pulled together and apart at the same time—the chick with the laughs. With a winning combination like that, how could anyone resist her?

Ms. Prentiss on the beginning—
"I was a student at Northwestern, and one day we were told that MGM was planning to hold a casting call for the film *Where the Boys Are*. Of course, all being theater-oriented, we whispered our reluctance to each other. But, sure enough, the very next day everyone had signed up. It so happened they were looking for a tall girl in particular, so I caught their attention. A short time later, they called to request a screen test."

the initial experience—
"I got the part, and signed a multi-year contract. I loved it. In those days they still took care of everything. I was very lucky."

an interesting anecdote—
"Even though I'm 5' 10", they still shot me standing on a box, with the camera positioned down low."

why she went into acting—
"I knew it would help me to figure out who I wanted to be as a person—like someone looking into a mirror for the first time and seeing their reflection, I wasn't sure what I saw of myself. And playing different characters has helped me to experience life more fully."

why we haven't seen more of her—
"I wanted to take care of my family the same way the studio took care of me, completely."

on life—
"Take from life's experiences and be interested in living. You may or may not like things, but life is always in a state of change—it's alive."

top
G O L D I E   H A W N
Born November 21, 1945, in Washington, D.C. Hawn's first job was as a chorus dancer at the New York World's Fair (1964). Her dancing talents came in handy when she was memorably cast in the ensemble variety series "Laugh-In." Her adorable, slightly kooky personality made her a favorite of the viewing audience and a natural for her first big, onscreen role, in *Cactus Flower* (1969), opposite powerhouses Ingrid Bergman and Walter Matthau. Ably holding her own (actually very nearly stealing the whole picture), Hawn won an Oscar and quickly established herself as a star of the big screen. A second nomination came for *Private Benjamin* (1980), with Hawn making a more significant impact as producer. Married twice, she has been romantically linked with actor Kurt Russell since the mid-1980s. (*Ken Whitmore/MPTV*)

bottom
B E T T E   M I D L E R
Born December 1, 1945, in Honolulu, Hawaii A skilled actress with a gift for bawdy humor and a melancholy singing voice. Bette had a bit part in the film *Hawaii* (1966) and played—first in the chorus, then as the eldest daughter—onstage in *Fiddler on the Roof*. Her popularity surged while appearing as a performer in the notorious gay establishment the Continental Baths in New York. The recordings that followed, under the moniker "The Divine Miss M" led to a Best New Artist Grammy in 1973 and a special Tony. In 1978, her television special won an Emmy. In 1979, she received another Grammy for Record of the Year for the title song from *The Rose*. Her heartbreaking lead role was nominated for a Best Actress Oscar (a second came for 1992's *One For the Boys*) and won her a notorious pair of Golden Globes. Today, admittedly "Disneyized" (owing to recent collaborations with the famed family studio), Midler nonetheless continues to wow them with her special brand of adult comedy. (*Peggy Sirota/Outline*)

far right
C A R O L   B U R N E T T
Born April 23, 1933, in San Antonio, Texas A multi-Emmy-award winner, Burnett's career kicked into high gear with her able comedic support on "The Gary Moore Show," during the late-'50s and early-'60s. Her success was parlayed into Broadway musicals, television variety specials (including the beginning of a long, collaborative effort with Julie Andrews) and finally, her own series, "The Carol Burnett Show." A dream showcase for Carol's delightful, rubber-faced hijinks, the show would last a remarkable eleven years in prime time. However, for whatever reason, the same level of acclaim was not repeated on film. Their loss. Winner of a landmark case against a powerful supermarket tabloid, she ably defended her stand on the accuracy of the written word and a star's right to some measure of guaranteed privacy. (*Gabi Rona/MPTV*)

left

M A E   W E S T

Born August 17, 1889, in Brooklyn, NY. Died 1980

In a time when women had limited authority, West wielded power almost without question. It helped that she was remarkably savvy, especially when it came to dialogue and the censors; if she hadn't been, her legend might never have come to be. Coming up through the ranks in vaudeville, she caused a sensation on Broadway with a number of vehicles, including *Sex* and *Diamond Lil'*. These successes caught the attention of Paramount and she was summoned westward. Although she appeared in only nine films during the thirties, her influence was profound; she was unabashedly sexy in a time when the word itself could rarely be spoken onscreen. "Retiring" from films in 1943, she ventured once again into stage performances, capped by a hugely successful nightclub act in the mid-'50s. Her last film was 1978's *Sextette*. (*Kobal*)

right

J E A N   H A R L O W

H a r l e a n   C a r p e n t e r

Born March 3, 1911, in Kansas City, Mo. Died 1937

It is remarkable that in so short an amount of time (twenty-six years), one individual could become so indelible in the public consciousness. But Harlow was an original, and when you take into account what her life was like, you can understand the adulation. This charmeuse-clad coquette was "discovered" by Howard Hughes (after a few years of bit parts) and set about becoming the first bonafide female sex symbol in sound films. *Dinner at Eight* (1934) is one of her most highly-regarded works, while *Bombshell* (1933) is great art imitating life. Watch them both. Because of her untimely demise (due to complications from uremic poisoning), many of the scenes in her last film, *Saratoga* (1934), were shot using a double from behind. The film was posthumously released to much success, owing to its particularly sensational nature. (*Author's collection*)

glamazon

JAYNE MANSFIELD
Vera Jayne Palmer
Born April 19, 1933, in Bryn Mawr, Pa. Died 1967
Given the way she was "used" onscreen,
it's a surprise to learn that Mansfield was
a drama student at both UCLA and the
University of Texas. I mention this not to
slight her talent (or determination), it just
seems that acting lessons were of no help
to her career. The second most famous
bombshell to come out of the fifties (Marilyn was, of course, first), Mansfield
endured the indignities that a career
based largely on physical attributes eventually wrought, and with its sharp decline
in the mid-'60s, she was vanquished to
low-budget "cheapies." (Regardless,
indulge yourself with her triumph, 1957's
Will Success Spoil Rock Hunter?, an amusing
Eisenhower-era novelty.) Adding insult to
injury, her death—a horrific decapitation
in an auto accident—was relished with
much the same vulgarity that would sur-
round her life. A Golden Globe winner, in
1956, as Most Promising Newcomer. (*Corbis-Bettmann*)

ANITA EKBERG
Born September 29, 1931, in Malmo, Sweden
A former Miss Sweden, this Scandinavian
goddess never made as "big" an impres-
sion in films as her ample endowments
would have allowed (even though she did
win a Most Promising Newcomer Golden
Globe in 1955). Regardless, she makes a
huge splash in Fellini's *La Dolce Vita* (1960).
(*Archive Photos*)

left

MARILYN MONROE

Norma Jean Mortenson

Born June 1, 1926, in Los Angeles, California. Died 1962
There have been many celluloid sex goddesses—long
before, during, and long after. Some have been more
beautiful, talented, became stars faster, possibly even
more vulnerable. So what made Monroe different?
Notably, much of this reverence came after her (highly speculative) demise; during her reign she was as
much pillaged as she was prized. That she should be
so popular today, nearly four decades after her death,
is a testament not only to the unique qualities she
brought to film, but to possibly our own need to
coddle the mistreated and assailable among us, especially those we forceably place upon a pedestal. It
should be noted that Marilyn did not go completely
unrewarded during her career and was the recipient
of a Golden Globe (as Best Actress) for her work in
Some Like it Hot (1959). (Ironically, her win did not
result in an Oscar nomination.) (*Richard Miller/MPTV*)

right

URSULA ANDRESS

Born March 19, 1936, in Bern, Switzerland
International screen sex symbol by way of her first
film hit, the Bond flick *Dr. No* (1962). After this
smash, which also unleashed Sean Connery, Andress
went on to appear in dozens of foreign (and few
domestic) pictures. A departure from your typical
voluptuous star, Andress had an underlying "don't
mess with me" aspect to her personality that made
her a formidable attraction. Married ten years to
actor John Derek, a man who knew his way with
beautiful women. (*Corbis-Bettmann*)

left

MARLENE DIETRICH
Maria Magdalene Dietrich
Born December 27, 1901, in Berlin, Germany. Died 1992
What is there left to say about this Teutonic temptress? Perhaps no star was as popular, despite the fact that very few of her films were enormous financial successes. Beginning with her infamous Von Sternberg collaboration (*The Blue Angel*, 1930), Dietrich's image was cultivated, molded, and contrived to a degree that the lines between fact and fiction became forever blurred. The general tenor of the legend, though, is undisputable. Her face and figure, so perfectly lit, are unmatchable—Garbo was the only other star of that era who could challenge her. In many ways, we have her to thank for aspects of female emancipation—her ambiguous, unapologetic sexuality and unabashed sense of style (no one looked better in pants). By the late-'50s, this "World's Most Glamourous Grandmother" (and she was) took ably to recording and concert appearances. One-time Oscar-nominee for *Morocco* (1930). (*Author's collection*)

right

AVA GARDNER
Born Dec. 24, 1922, in Grabton, NC. Died 1990
What a Christmas present! A breathtaking, "Venusian" star who really came into her own in the late-1940s through mid-'50s (especially effective in full-color). This "goddess of love" was married to Mickey Rooney (if you can believe it), Artie Shaw, and Frank Sinatra. Not surprisingly, this popular pepperpot was once deemed "The World's Most Beautiful Woman." No one carried off a pencil skirt, high heels, and red lipstick better than this raven-haired dame! Besides her multiple physical assets, she proved to be quite a capable actress, too, in *Mogambo* (1953, AAN), *Barefoot Contessa* (1954), and *Night of the Iguana* (1964), among others. (*Archive Photos*)

enchantress

LANA TURNER

Julia Jean Mildred Frances Turner
Born February 8, 1920, in Wallace, Idaho. Died 1998
One of the few stars who, it can be said, was born in true Hollywood legendary fashion. Upon arriving in Los Angeles with her widowed mother (her father was murdered during a robbery), high-school-aged Lana was spotted enjoying a soda at Schwab's drugstore by a newspaper editor, who passed his discovery on to director Mervyn LeRoy. At the time, she was also wearing a clingy sweater—the look served her well—she was, from thereon, known as "The Sweater Girl." Going from the forties, fifties, and into much of the sixties, her roles covered a range of flirtatious ingenues to mature madames, though her career was never well-respected. Few times was she ever as good, or better, than her scripted material; one occasion being *Peyton Place* (1957), for which she received an Oscar nomination. Her films are known more for their sheer melodramatic entertainment value; witness one of her biggest hits, *Imitation of Life* (1959). Like many Hollywood vixens, Lana's private life was also not without incident. Married seven times, including Artie Shaw and actor Lex Barker, her relationship with hoodlum Johnny Stompanato ended with his stabbing death at the hands of Lana's daughter Cheryl Crane. Controversy still surrounds the actual circumstances. (*Kobal*)

bottom

HEDY LAMARR

Hedwig Eva Maria Kiesler
Born November 9, 1913, in Vienna, Austria
Though she was promoted as the world's most beautiful woman upon her Hollywood debut (in *Algiers*) in 1938, Lamarr was never so superlative in terms of box office grosses. Interestingly, her most remarkable achievement may be offscreen, when she codeveloped a signal-jamming device used by the Allies in WWII. She has also often been accused of kleptomania. Nevertheless, starting from her prurient 1933 Czech film *Ecstacy* to today, she is still considered one of the screen's most lovely ladies. (*Kobal*)

far right

GRETA GARBO

Greta Louisa Gustafsson
Born September 18, 1905, in Stockholm, Sweden. Died 1990
From the beginning, and through her death at age eighty-four, Garbo was one of the few (if possibly the only) screen star who never once had to come from behind the veil of mystery that surrounded her to remain in the public consciousness. And she was, for her entire adult life (though her professional career lasted only about nineteen years—in earnest, just twelve). Four times nominated for an Oscar, she never won, an error that was "corrected" with an honorary award in 1954. (She, of course, did not attend.) Considered one of the screen's most beguilingly beautiful women, with her somber stare and sinking shoulders, Garbo passed away with an amazing "fortune" intact—both in her own personal wealth (coming from abject poverty) and the films she left behind (like 1937's *Camille*) for an ever-adoring public. (*Kobal*)

RITA HAYWORTH
Margarita Carmen Cansino
Born October 17, 1918, in Brooklyn, New York. Died 1987

This most glamourous of female stars was a professional dancer from age twelve. As a chorine in the mid-'30s, she danced her way through a series of B pictures, using her real name. Renamed Rita and her hair dyed red, things began to simmer, coming to a full boil in the early '40s. A Columbia studio fave, she was unrivaled in terms of public adoration and the box office. Unfortunately, Rita was a naughty girl and frequently got herself into trouble—typically the male kind. (This carousing impacted the amount and quality of her films.) Married five times, including to Prince Aly Khan, Orson Welles, and singer Dick Haymes, she often "overlapped" her relationships. Sadly, at the time of her death, a long bout with Alzheimer's disease left her a faint shadow of her former lovely self. To recall her in her heyday, watch *Cover Girl* (1944) and *Gilda* (1946). (*Corbis-Bettmann*)

DOROTHY DANDRIDGE
Born November 9, 1923, in Cleveland, Ohio. Died 1965

Dorothy's career is historically significant, if, for no other reason, that she became the first African American female nominated for a Best Actress Oscar for her fiery portrayal of Carmen in Otto Preminger's 1954 film *Carmen Jones*. (Interestingly, though she had a divine voice, her singing was dubbed.) A stunner who, despite her talents—acting, singing, and dancing—was underutilized by a town that couldn't cope with her color and the fact that she could attract a white male audience. Tragically, her work and financial standing always suffered because of this dilemma (once losing all she had in a get-rich-quick scheme). Unable to deal with the possibly insurmountable obstacles, she took her own life with an overdose of barbiturates (ironically, just before she was to begin a New York nightclub engagement). Given her skills, one cannot help but speculate on what the outcome of her career would be had she been born just a few years later. (*Bob Willoughby/MPTV*)

left
SOPHIA LOREN
Sofia Scicolone
Born September 20, 1934, in Rome, Italy
Loren became one of the few international female stars who proved her acting mettle with a gut-wrenching role in *Two Woman* (1962); it won her the Academy Award. (It also marked the first time that a statuette was given for a performance in a foreign language.) The film, in one way, also mirrored Loren's own hardship-ridden early life in poverty-stricken, wartorn Italy. It is miraculous that she survived and became so beloved (and lovely). After appearing in numerous beauty contests throughout Italy, she came to the attention of producer Carlo Ponti; he became her svengali. By the mid-'50s, Loren was an international sensation. However, few Hollywood-made films have been able to capture the earthy essence of this screen siren, so it comes as no surprise that her great successes lie in work made abroad. This proud mother of two gorgeous sons netted a second Oscar nomination for *Marriage Italian Style* (1964). A fabulous quote: "Everything you see, I owe to spaghetti." (*Corbis-Bettmann*)

right
GINA LOLLOBRIGIDA
Born July 4, 1927, in Subiaco, Italy
One of the screen's most glamourous and vivacious stars. Lovingly nicknamed "La Lollo" by European audiences, Gina was kept from Hollywood in the early '50s by a dispute with then film producer Howard Hughes. Eventually, with obstacles overcome, she soared to prominence with stateside moviegoers as well. However, few films proved a match for her "larger-than-life," fiery screen personality. Fortunately, Lollobrigida never lacked for outside interests, including a passion for photography. Appeared for one season on television's "Falcon Crest" (1984). (*Corbis-Bettmann*)

Hollywood

A FAWCETT PUBLICATION

5¢

OCTOBER

DOROTHY LAMOUR
Photographed by Kahle

MORE NEWS ABOUT FILM FOLK THAN ANY OTHER MAGAZINE
STORIES ABOUT BETTE DAVIS · GEORGE RAFT · DOROTHY LAMOUR

left
DEBRA PAGET
Debralee Griffin
Born August 19, 1933, in Denver, Colorado
Once linked romantically to Elvis Presley
(he gave her a jewel-encrusted car), a
delectable Paget never became a top-
notch film star, despite attempts by
directors as unlikely as Fritz Lang and
Cecil B. DeMille (*The Ten Commandments*,
1956). Possibly she was too pretty (and
short, even by Hollywood standards), to
be taken seriously as an actress. Her
third marriage from 1964–71, to the oil-
man nephew of China's Madame Chiang
Kai-Shek, effectively ended her career.
(*Corbis-Bettmann*)

right
DOROTHY LAMOUR
Mary Leta Dorothy Kaumeyer
Born Dec. 10, 1914, in New Orleans, La. Died 1996
An enduring and endearing star, who is
best recalled wearing a sarong and most
often remembered for her seven screen
appearances opposite Bob Hope and Bing
Crosby in their "Road" picture series.
(*Author's collection*)

soubrette

ANNE FRANCIS

Born September 16, 1930, in Ossining, New York Superstardom may never have been in the cards for this twinkly-eyed, beauty-marked darling, but Anne did achieve a measure of TV immortality for her short-lived work (and cool outfits) as Honey West, in the same-named series (1966–67). She also pops up in a number of interesting, diverse films and roles, including the ingenue lead (*Forbidden Planet*, 1956), pretty bit player (*Portrait of Jennie*, 1948), or seasoned showgirl (*Funny Girl*, 1968). A child model and actress, this cutie was once dubbed "The Little Queen of Soap Opera." (*Corbis-Bettmann*)

left

B A R B A R A   E D E N

B a r b a r a   J e a n   H u f f m a n

A dreamy Eden started out as a singer, played leading parts in feature films (*Five Weeks in a Balloon*, 1962, etc.), but found greatest success by popping out of a bottle in the longplaying sitcom "I Dream of Jeannie" (1965–70). As a mystical denizen of Cocoa Beach, Florida, Eden's character was not without controversy: censors made it a point of not allowing her navel to show in her harem costume. My, how far we've come. (*Archive Photos*)

right

A N G I E   D I C K I N S O N

A n g e l i n e   B r o w n

Born September 30, 1931, in Kulm, North Dakota

A beauty contest winner who found her way to Hollywood in the mid-'50s. Played starlet bit parts, until a big break came along with the female lead in *Rio Bravo* (1959). Though movies never adequately showcased this flaxen-haired lovely (an exception being her late entry *Dressed to Kill*, 1980), at least her starring (and Emmy-nominated) role as Detective Pepper in television's "Police Woman" (1974–78) will secure her a place in the pantheon of bodacious babes. (*MPTV*)

Is there anyone sexier than Angie Dickinson? Even as a gay kid I knew she was a babe. When we talked, I found out she was the sweetest and funniest person, too. What more could you want?

Angie Dickinson on what she wanted to be—
"A movie star. As a kid I was a ham, and loved to perform for my relatives. In early photographs my sisters looked shy and reserved—I was always smiling, bubbly, beaming. I knew it was my calling, but only if I could cut the mustard and had the talent. I would never want to climb a mountain if I knew I was going to fall off."

what girls today want to be—
"They want to be stars, too, but not movie stars. In my day, they were considered extremely special, you revered them. It's different now."

her longrunning series—
"I had always done a lot of television. When this came along I was very hesitant. Then someone said to me, 'Don't you want to be a household name?' That was the clincher."

any regrets about her decision—
"Am I glad I did it? Yes, but it is a close call. It was very rough. But unfortunately, you can't take both forks in a road."

being a sex symbol—
"I think of myself as a sexy actress, not a sex symbol. I've always wanted the focus to be on my body of work, not my body (of measurements)—but I am flattered to be thought of as one."

on sex in films—
"It's all in how it is presented artistically or blatantly. On film, though, I find a person in a towel more interesting than one without."

on life—
"I'm like a lot of people, I want to have my cake and eat it, too—I don't work enough and don't want to work too much."

James J.
Kriegsmann
N.Y.

ANN-MARGRET
Anne Margret Olson "Miss Kitten with a Whip" began her career in the spotlight on "Ted Mack's Amateur Hour" when she was just sixteen. Her screen debut followed shortly thereafter in the Capra remake of *Pocketful of Miracles* (1961). Her success in *Bye, Bye Birdie* (1963) endeared her to a teen audience and launched her into years of youthful, sexpot roles—and a lot of groovy dance moves! Her talents, fortunately, allowed her a turnaround with an acclaimed performance in Mike Nichols' *Carnal Knowledge* (1971). It could be said that the role saved her career. It and her work in *Tommy* (1975) were both Oscar-nominated (for Best Supporting Actress and Best Actress). A famed nightclub performer, though not without perilous incident, she has been married to actor Roger Smith since 1967, who has acted as her personal manager ever since. Included in her resume is one Top-20 music hit: "I Just Don't Understand," from 1961. (*Archive Photos*)

left

BRIGITTE BARDOT
Born September 28, 1934, in Paris
Though some ardent feminists may want to disagree, Bardot could be solely responsible for bringing female sexuality (on film) out of the dark ages. Her "sex kitten" image, which she has never been particularly fond of, was new to moviegoers in the mid-'50s. Aided by her then-husband Roger Vadim, "BB's" worldwide popularity gave adult "art" films a much needed boost and a measure of respectability (especially given how the category has digressed over the years). Now, almost a mythic figure in her homeland, Bardot still resides in Paris and finds solace in the care and protection of animals. A French Legion of Honor winner in 1985. Her most important film: *And God Created Woman* (1956). (*Archive Photos*)

right

CANDICE BERGEN
Born May 8, 1946, in Beverly Hills, California
With her unique, somewhat clipped style of acting, Bergen rose to major stardom, though not necessarily through films (though she enjoyed great success in *Carnal Knowledge* and an Oscar nomination for *Starting Over* in 1979), but via her longrunning sitcom "Murphy Brown" (1988–98). Her title role netted her an unprecedented five Emmys; the show also won the prestigious Peabody in 1991. Daughter of famed ventriloquist Edgar Bergen. Long married to the late director Louis Malle. (*Archive Photos*)

far left
TUESDAY WELD
Susan Ker Weld
Born August 27, 1943, in New York City, NY
When she started out in films (at thirteen) she played ingenues with a sexy edge. (How could she not be with a provocative name like Tuesday?) This continued through the mid-'60s. All the while her private life was hell, starting with a nervous breakdown way back at age nine, and an attempted suicide by the ripe old age of twelve. (It is unfortunate, but relevant, to note that she was supporting her family from the age of three, beginning as a model.) Fortunately, roles like that in *Pretty Poison* (1968), saved her career from extinction. By the time she was nominated for an Oscar in 1977 (for her supporting role in *Looking For Mr. Goodbar*), Weld's career had gone through a metamorphosis; a book no longer judged by its cover. (*Everett*)

near left
CLAUDIA CARDINALE
Born April 15, 1939, in Tunis
Though molded in the image of Loren and Lollobrigida, Cardinale was not able to attain quite the same international star stature of her comely compatriots. Still, this stacked stunner never lacked for work, although one would be hard-pressed to find many noteworthy film undertakings stateside. Nevertheless, in recent years, she has taken ably to producing many of her own films. (*Curt Gunther/MPTV*)

top

FARRAH FAWCETT

Born February 2, 1946, in Corpus Christi, Texas
During the mid-'70s, unless you lived under a rock, the image of this exuberant beauty was unavoidable. Her pin-up poster stands as among the most popular and memorable cultural icons of the postwar era. Beyond that bit of ephemera, she is most-recalled as one third of the original triad in the pubescent tele-teaser, "Charlie's Angels," playing Jill Munroe. Never a critic's favorite, she delivered some mid-'80s powerhouse performances in *Extremities* and *The Burning Bed*. (*Bruce McBroom/MPTV*)

bottom

SUZANNE PLESHETTE

Born January 31, 1937, in New York City, New York
Whether playing queen-bee Leona Helmsley (in a television melodrama), an American tourist (in the light comedy *If It's Tuesday, This Must Be Belgium*, 1969), a stalwart mate (on the longrunning series "The Bob Newhart Show"), or an ex-girlfriend destined to meet a frenzied, feathered end (in *The Birds*, 1963), Suzanne has had a long career that only fleetingly uses her to her best advantage. Married very briefly (nine months) to actor Troy Donahue in 1964. (*Archive Photos*)

far right

JOAN COLLINS

Born March 23, 1933, in London
Some people get no respect, as an assessment of Joan's professional career will attest. Vainly, though earnestly, trying for stardom throughout the fifties and sixties, Collins had to settle for the status of also-ran. Sultry and sinister, but stunning nonetheless, with few exceptions in mostly unexceptional films—*The Girl on the Velvet Swing* (1955) and *The Opposite Sex* (1956)—Collins had to wait until the eighties rise of the primetime soap opera for her day in the sun. As the scheming temptress Alexis Carrington, Joan redefined the character you "loved to hate" and made millions out of bellicose bitchery (she also got an Emmy nomination). Still fabulous today, the older sister of novelist Jackie Collins is herself a best-selling writer. *Author's note: If just sheer numbers are indicative of something, though I can't articulate what that might be, Collins is truly a star among stars. The photographic material I found to represent Joan placed her easily in fourth place behind such stellar company as Marilyn, Elizabeth, and Audrey. No simple feat. (*Corbis-Bettmann*)

left

ANNA MAY WONG

Wong   Liu   Tsong

Born January 3, 1907, in Los Angeles, Ca. Died 1961

Were it not for a 1920s interest in the Orient, Wong may never have become a major film star. However because of a worldwide fascination with Asian culture, she did. Still, as it was, it did not keep her from being used in a way that today would be considered inappropriate. Her two most famous films, nonetheless, are, as a slave girl, in *The Thief of Bagdad* (1925), and opposite Marlene Dietrich in *Shanghai Express* (1930). How gorgeous the two were. (*Kobal*)

right

LUPE   VELEZ

Maria Guadalupe Velez de Villalobos

Born July 18, 1908, in San Luis Potosi, Mexico. Died 1944

One of the few times where an actress' off- and onscreen personas were in complete synch with each other. Velez, known (derogatorily) as the "Mexican Spitfire," was as volatile in real life as her film incarnations, even given that many of her roles were based on flagrant racial stereotyping. Though convent educated, Lupe was never the passive type, and her many love affairs were well publicized, including those with Gary Cooper and Johnny Weismuller, whom she would marry. She even staged her suicide death. She made sure to have her hair and makeup done and the room trimmed with flowers before ingesting a lethal dose of pills. (*Author's collection*)

sugar&spice

CARMEN MIRANDA
Maria do Carmo Miranda da Cunha
Born February 9, 1909, near Lisbon, Portugal. Died 1955
Is it a coincidence that a woman renowned for her nuts-and-berry-encrusted headdresses would have a father who was a fruit wholesaler? The world may never know. However, this most outlandish and delectable screen personality, aka "The Brazilian Bombshell," enlivened many a forties musical with her swaying incantations and colorful regalia. By the fifties, though, her flamboyant style was out of favor. Nevertheless, her sudden death (frighteningly portended with a collapse on live television) was mourned by the world, particularly by her homeland. A museum in Rio commemorates her memory. (*Kobal*)

DOLORES DEL RIO
Lolita Dolores Martinez Asunsolo Lopez Negrette
Born August 3, 1905, in Durango, Mexico. Died 1983
Even though she was absolutely exquisite, Dolores' stunning good looks did not help her avoid typecasting. When she appeared in sound films, the problem was magnified; now her dark beauty was matched by an accent, making it all but impossible to cast her in anything but exotic, ethnic roles. Painful as the experience must have been, Del Rio stayed in Hollywood until the mid-'40s. By then, she made the wise career move to star in (and share in the profits of) Mexican-made films. The multi-year contract resulted in much of her best work, though little of it was seen north of the border. At one time this aristocratic-born, second cousin to silent film star Ramon Novarro, was married to acclaimed set designer Cedric Gibbons. (*Kobal*)

RITA MORENO
Rosita Dolores Alverio
Born December 11, 1931, in Humacao, Puerto Rico
Winner of the quadruple crown of entertainment—the Oscar, Tony, Emmy (two), and Grammy. Starting on Broadway at age thirteen, through small-ish parts, playing the exotic in a hefty handful of films, including *Singin' in the Rain* (1952) and *The King and I* (1956), her breakout performance as Anita in *West Side Story* (1961), to delightful stints on television's "The Electric Company" and "The Muppet Show," Moreno is an indefatigable entertainment force, and we love it. Today, busy at work on the controversial and acclaimed show "Oz". (*Corbis-Bettmann*)

No one has the energy or a love of life like Rita Moreno. Her passion shows in everything she has ever done. She is an inspiration to us all.

For Rita Moreno, where did it all start?
"As a little girl in Puerto Rico, I would always dance for my Grandfather—I was always shaking my booty, doing the salsa. I felt like a born entertainer."

then what?
"I moved to New York, which was very rough—you had to scramble. It was very much sink or swim. I chose to swim."

and next?
"In school, no matter what the show was, you could always find me, Rosita, doing her Mexican hat dance. I had to find other opportunities. So I got a part in an independent film, *So Young , So Bad*, playing a Latina girl, directed by Paul Henreid. But I wanted to be a real movie star, like the ones in MGM musicals. I got there just in time to meet them all—that great stable of actors they had."

when did she know she had made it?
"Certainly, not at the time. Even when I won (for *West Side Story*) I knew nothing about its effect on the Hispanic community. I was told many years later there was cheering in Spanish Harlem. I never knew any of this, because Hispanic people do not write fan letters. Now I know the influence my career had and am very proud of my contribution."

what about race in films?
"When I started working, my race was not considered a good thing, it limited you—you were percieved as inferior. Things are changing rapidly now. Today a Latina role wouldn't have terrible dialogue like, "You no love Ula?""

and the future of films?
"There is a profound need for the ingenious, and we need more small pictures; an actor doesn't get lost in a small film."

Before an exquisite Nancy Kwan burst onto the scene in the early-1960s, she had already been turning heads (and pirouettes) as a ballerina, most notably with the Royal Ballet in London. (Incidentally, dancing was, and remains, one of her passions.) But her entrance into films was happenstance. Kwan often travelled back home (to Hong Kong) for the holidays. On one particular occasion she went to visit her uncle, an architect in the film business, at a studio he had helped to build. That particular day, producer Ray Stark and company were conducting part of their worldwide search for talent for his upcoming film version of the bestseller, *The World of Suzie Wong*. Gathered in the large room were many beautiful young hopefuls, but it was Kwan, comfortably sitting in a chair observing the proceedings, who caught their eye. Mr. Stark asked the unassuming young Kwan if she'd be interested in going to Los Angeles to make a test. "I was very young, but the idea excited me; it would be a chance to see America." Getting her parents' consent, she left for California.

Though the test was considered a success, Kwan learned that the part of "Suzie" would go to France Nuyen (who originated it on Broadway). Undaunted, she consoled herself by taking the same role in the national touring company. Then, not too long after, she recieved yet another call and another request for a screen test, only this time it was to be with William Holden (the male lead of the picture) and would take place in London. Heading back to England a bit confused but nonetheless anxious, Kwan soon found out that Nuyen was no longer with the picture, for that matter, neither was the original director. The test took place, and proved the charm—chemistry between the two was obvious. The most coveted role for an Asian actress—before, during, or since—was hers.

Those first heady months were not without amusing revelations, as Kwan noted, "Making a movie was not always as exciting as I thought it would be. You sit around all day, then shoot a few minutes here…a few minutes there. You do interiors, then exteriors. The process is all in bits and pieces, so you don't always get a sense of the whole thing." But being where she was came with its own rewards, "I was at a cocktail party when I was introduced to Ross Hunter, who said to me, 'you are Linda Lo.' That's how I got my next part in *Flower Drum Song*. Oh, to be in the right place at the right time."

Being Eurasian myself (of Korean and German American parentage), I was particularly interested in knowing what Ms. Kwan's real life was like, then and now. Growing up, she played an important (albeit subtle) part in my own self-perception. I was not surprised to learn from her that many other Eurasians (and Asians, alike) felt the same way. Flattered and a bit humbled by the notoriety, she says, "Being thought of as a 'role model' wasn't something I was fully aware of while it was happening. Now I'm beginning to realize what my presence meant to people—it is such a responsibility." But being so prominent had its drawbacks, too. "Some people are angry with me, because they blame my playing the role of a prostitute in such a popular film with reinforcing a stereotype of Asian women as wanton. But what choice did I have? Not to do it? It was a very important part." I agree, as individuals (and as a culture) we have the power to decide what course our own lives take. But did she herself run into problems because of her race? "For me, I felt very lucky. No one said anything to my face, but I don't know what went on behind my back," and of her singular career, "I was under contract and ended up playing different ethnic parts (other than purely Asian women), something I couldn't do now because it wouldn't be politically correct. But I learned a lot doing them, even from doing bad pictures. However, to sustain a career you must have the roles and they weren't being written. Today it is not much better; there are still not enough good roles for Asian women."

She is quite moving when she gives her thoughts on herself being Eurasian, and advice for those in similar circumstances, "Sometimes it is like sitting between two chairs—not feeling comfortable in either. But I have always tried to make the most of it; bridging two cultures gives you a very special perspective on life—the chance to see it from two different sides" and her philosophy on living, "I take things as they come, I feel the joys in life should be taken from the journey not in the goals."

NANCY KWAN
Born May 19, 1939 in Hong Kong Of Chinese-English parentage, a divinely beautiful Kwan suffered in an industry that had no place for her ethnicity. Like Anna Mae Wong many years before, to her contemporaries, Miyoshi Umeki and France Nuyen, Kwan was given little opportunity to flex her acting muscles. Nevertheless, *The World of Suzie Wong* (1960) with William Holden, was an international hit, and subsequent appearances in *Flower Drum Song* (1961) and *Fate is the Hunter* (1964) prove her an engaging screen presence. (*Wallace Seawell/MPTV*)

left

BARBARA STANWYCK

R u b y S t e v e n s

Born July 16, 1907, in Brooklyn, New York. Died 1990
Stanwyck, once she became a film star,
excelled in playing heroines struggling to
surmount the odds (even many of her
comedic characters were surrounded by
much the same untoward conditions).
She was also renowned for her dedica-
tion, professionalism, and hardwork. Her
resolve must have been influenced by a
troubled childhood; she was orphaned at
age four and lived from place to place.
Four Oscar nominations (for *Stella Dallas*,
1937, *Ball of Fire*, 1941, *Double Indemnity*,
1944, and *Sorry, Wrong Number*, 1948)
never ended in a win, but she did collect
three Emmys, including one for the television miniseries "The Thorn Birds," in
1983. Married to actor Robert Taylor,
from 1939 to 1951. (*Kobal*)

right

ANN SOTHERN

H a r r i e t t e L a k e

Born Jan. 22, 1909, in Valley City, N.D.
Hardworking, likeable, underrated star
who neatly straddled high- and low-end
pictures in a career that lasted well over
five decades. Starting as a singer, she land-
ed her first bit part in a 1929 musical,
relocated to Broadway, then returned to
Hollywood in 1933 and began working
for Columbia. In 1939, she switched to
MGM and starred in her first (of ten)
"Maisie" films: a series of B movies cen-
tered around the exploits of a heart-of-
gold blond. Throughout the forties she
also popped up in such highly regarded
works as *Lady Be Good* (1941) and *A Letter to Three Wives* (1949). The fifties saw
her successfully crossover into television,
headlining two series: "Private Secretary"
and "The Ann Sothern Show." By 1987,
after innumerable appearances on the big
and small screens, Sothern received her
first (and only) Oscar nomination for *The
Whales of August*. (*Author's collection*)

doll & dame

top
ANN SHERIDAN
Clara Lou Sheridan
Born February 21, 1915, in Denton, Texas. Died 1967
The screen's "Oomph" girl, so named as part of a
Warner Bros. publicity campaign. It did the trick,
making Sheridan a star. She reached her zenith in the
forties, with a combination of comedies, dramas, and
musicals. One of her best roles was as wife to Ronald
Reagan in *King's Row* (1942). (*Kobal*)

middle, left
SUSAN HAYWARD
Edythe Marrener
Born June 30, 1918, in Brooklyn, New York. Died 1975
With her upturned nose and trademark sneer, Hayward turned in a string of powerful characterizations
playing women involved in melodramatic situations—
alcoholism was a favorite. In real life things seemed
just as hard—a suicide attempt and her death from a
brain tumor. Five times nominated for an Oscar, she
won for her poignant portrayal of a death-row
inmate in *I Want to Live!* (1958), though she has always
felt her role in *I'll Cry Tomorrow* (1956) was her finest
hour. However, to film cultists, her mocking, self-
absorbed Helen Lawson in 1967's *Valley of the Dolls* is
the *piece de resistance*. (*Kobal*)

middle, right
GLORIA GRAHAME
Born November 28, 1924, in Los Angeles, California. Died 1981
One of the screen's baddest "bad" girls. Grahame
appeared in diverse roles, but all her best parts have
a common thread—a woman of unchecked desire.
Two of them were Oscar-nominated, *Crossfire* (1947)
and *The Bad and the Beautiful* (1952), winning for the
latter for her portrayal of a straying wife who meets
her demise. Sulkily attractive, with a slight, lispish
voice, Gloria stayed a major star only a few years
after her award-winning triumph. (*Corbis-Bettmann*)

bottom
MAUREEN O'HARA
Maureen FitzSimons
Born August 17, 1920, in Millwall, Ireland
Copper-haired colleen, whose first taste of fame
came at the hands of actor Charles Laughton, who
imported Maureen to star opposite him in *The
Hunchback of Notre Dame* (1939). In 1941, she
appeared in *How Green Was My Valley* (Best Picture,
1941) for director John Ford. Divine in everything
from swashbucklers to westerns, O'Hara is a delight,
too, in such classic family fare as *Miracle on 34th Street*
(1947), and *The Parent Trap* (1961). (*Paul Hesse/MPTV*)

far right
ARLENE DAHL
Born August 11, 1924, in Minneapolis, Minnesota
This divine doll was the Rhinegold beer girl of 1946.
For the most part, Dahl's film's were just an excuse
to display their glamourous star, though on occasion
she did get to break free of the trappings. Upon
actively retiring from movies, she became a well
regarded beauty columnist. Mother of actor Lorenzo
Lamas, by then-husband Fernando. (*Corbis-Bettmann*)

CYD CHARISSE

Tula Eunice Finklea
Born March 8, 1921, in Amarillo, Texas
Lovely, leggy brunette who started ballet
as a child, joining the Ballets Russe at age
thirteen, Under contract to MGM in the
mid-forties, she (literally) stood out as an
able dancing partner in a slew of noteworthy musicals, sometimes only as a featured dancer, as in the scene from *Singin'
in the Rain* (1952). Though she has
attempted the occasional dramatic role, it
is upon those glorious stems that she
achieved incomparable movie magic. Married to singer Tony Martin since 1948.
(*Corbis-Bettmann*)

ALICE FAYE

Alice Jean Leppert
Born May 5, 1912, in New York City, NY. Died 1999
A smooth contralto who was responsi-
ble for bringing us the magnificent music
standard "You'll Never Know" (from
Hello, Frisco Hello, 1943). Early in her
career, she was a band singer with Rudy
Vallee, then under contract to Fox,
where she became a huge musical star.
However, constant disagreements with
studio head Darryl Zanuck led to her
inevitable downfall. (His idea to bring in
Betty Grable to usurp her throne was
partially instrumental in her early retirement from film—that, and a severe bomb
with the drama *Fallen Angel* (1945). (*Private collection*)

muse

top

GINGER ROGERS
Virginia Katherine McMath
Born on July 16, 1911, in Independence, Missouri. Died 1995
Guided by her mother, Rogers worked her way up from the vaudeville circuit to become, unarguably, the feminine half of the most-adored dancing duo in Tinseltown. Her partner, of course, was Fred Astaire, and their work together helped a Depression-weary audience forget their troubles. They appeared in ten films together, including the Deco-delight *Top Hat* (1935). A quite dependable light dramatic actress, she garnered an Oscar for her work in *Kitty Foyle* (1940). Into the sixties, she successfully took over stage roles in *Hello, Dolly!* and *Mame*. Five times married, including to actor Lew Ayres and Jacques Bergerac. (*Kobal*)

bottom

ANN MILLER
Lucille Ann Collier
Born April 12, 1919, in Chireno, Texas
Underused in the beginning of her career (starting in the late-'30s), Miller shown brilliantly when given the spotlight—and a pair of tap shoes. An able actress, Ann's best work, nonetheless, seem relegated to her dancing vignettes, most notably in *Kiss Me Kate* (1953). Not surprisingly, her film career ended at about the same time MGM's output of musicals hit the skids. However, in her '60s, Miller delighted theatergoers with her still adept tapping in the long-touring show *Sugar Babies*. (*Kobal*)

far right

BETTY GRABLE
Elizabeth Ruth Grable
Born December 18, 1916 in St. Louis, Missouri. Died 1973
Several accounts give Grable's start in the chorus of Hollywood films at age twelve; she was no older than thirteen. Despite this early foray, it would be years before she became a star. By 1940, some ten years later, she was at Fox studios, and her appearance in their Technicolor musicals proved a magical combination. So attainably beautiful was she in face and body (especially those million-dollar-insured legs) that these physical attributes (and a modicum of talent) made her the highest-paid film performer of the mid-'40s. And it was on those fabled gams that she was also pegged the most popular "pin-up" of WW II. By the mid-'50s, though, she and Hollywood were finished with each other, and Grable, at the time married to band leader Harry James, turned to nightclubs and stage appearances. (*Archive Photos*)

far left, top
ELEANOR POWELL
Born Nov. 21, 1910, in Springfield, Mass. Died 1982
Quite possibly the best tap dancer in films. Powell worked her spell in just over a dozen movies, until interest in her forte waned considerably, forcing an abrupt end to her career. Married from 1943 to 1959 to actor Glenn Ford, upon their divorce she mounted a successful (though short-lived) return to dancing via a nightclub act. (*Kobal*)

far left, middle
JULIET PROWSE
Born Sept. 25, 1936, in Bombay, India. Died 1996
Raised in South Africa, Juliet made a splash in films (and with her costar, Frank Sinatra; they became engaged but never married) starting with *Can-Can*, 1960. However, this dazzling dervish made few movies, and most of them unworthy of her twirling talent. However, she did have her own mid-'60s television show, "Mona McCluskey." A leading arbiter and driving force for competitive ballroom dancing up to the time of her untimely death. (*Photofest*)

far left, bottom
VERA-ELLEN
Vera-Ellen Westmeyr Rohe
Born Feb. 16, 1926, in Cincinnati, Oh. Died 1981
Impossibly thin dancing star of the mid-1940s to mid-'50s. She had the look of someone who could snap in half at any moment, and her figure would certainly come under much scrutiny today. Regardless, she was charming, to say the least, and was a formidable dance partner for Astaire, Kelly, and Kaye. A most famous musical number, albeit short on dancing: probably "Sisters" with Rosemary Clooney, in *White Christmas* (1954). (*Corbis-Bettmann*)

near left
MITZI GAYNOR
Francesca Mitzi Gerber
Born Sept. 4, 1930, in Chicago, Illinois
A wide-eyed dancing delight. In a number of musicals, even Mitzi's inescapable charms did little to make her boffo at the registers. Regardless, *There's No Business Like Show Business* (1954), *Les Girls* (1957) and *South Pacific* (1958) offer up some marvelous moments to fans. Her eventual turn to nightclubs and television would prove to be much more successful venues for this charmer. (*Corbis-Bettmann*)

125

near right

LENA HORNE

Born June 30, 1917, in Brooklyn, New York

Horne is a survivor. This ravishing beauty (who, at one time, referred to herself as a sepia Hedy Lamarr) rose to psuedo-stardom in the mid-'40s as a featured performer in MGM musicals (though often cleverly relegated to solo vignettes that could be edited out of versions headed South), after years of plying her craft in nightclubs (most notably The Cotton Club), only to be an outcast (because of her association with actor Paul Robeson) during the 1950s blacklisting. However, she did continue to work during this period, and recorded her classic album *Porgy and Bess* in 1959. A most exquisite song stylist, her longtime efforts would finally pay off in 1981, with the astounding success of her one-woman show, Lena Horne: The Lady and Her Music; garnering a smash worldwide tour, a Grammy, and a Tony. (*Kobal*)

far right, top

PEARL BAILEY

Born March 29, 1918, in Newport News, Va. Died 1990

Underused, as so many African American singer-actresses are, Bailey nevertheless fashioned a legendary life for herself that included being named U.S. delegate to the United Nations. A preacher's daughter, Bailey's few film appearances include *Carmen Jones* (1954) and *The Landlord* (1970). She also recieved a special Tony for her title role in the 1967 all-black version of *Hello, Dolly!* Also, a 1988 Medal of Freedom winner, and, at age 67, she completed a degree in theology at Georgetown University. (*Wallace Seawell/MPTV*)

far right, bottom

JEANETTE MACDONALD

Born June 18, 1901, in Philadelphia, Penn. Died 1965

An operatic singing sensation, who became one half of "America's Sweetheart's" when she teamed with Nelson Eddy. Jeanette's popularity was enormous, but even her musical charms could not carry her through the war, and her contract with MGM ended in 1942. Though today they are a bit too sweet to endure, her films are an interesting glimpse at a world long since gone. (*Kobal*)

far left
BETTY HUTTON
Betty June Thornburg
Born February 26, 1921, in Battle Creek, Michigan
Though Hutton was already a popular musical star, her replacing Judy Garland in screen version of *Annie Get Your Gun* (1950) was the opportunity of a lifetime; she made the most of it. She then starred in DeMille's *The Greatest Show on Earth* (Best Picture, 1952), but abruptly ended her film career by walking out on her contract. (She insisted her then-husband direct all her subsequent movies.) Attempts to make a comeback never caught fire. Years later, she was found working as a cook in a Catholic rectory, having gone through an entire $10 million dollar fortune. (*Sid Avery/MPTV*)

near left
DINAH SHORE
Frances Rose Shore
Born March 1, 1917, in Winchester, Tenn. Died 1994
An enormously successful singing star, beginning in the late-1930s, Shore was not successful on the big screen. Though it hardly mattered, and it never affected her popularity. She was better suited to the intimacy of the small screen and was a decades-long standard, whether hosting her early variety series or an informal chat. It helped that she could count among her frequent guests the biggest names in show business. Winner of three Emmys. (*Sid Avery/MPTV*)

right
ROSEMARY CLOONEY
Born May 23, 1928, in Maysville, Kentucky
Her hugely successful recording career began with the delectable "Come-on-a-My-House" through "Hey, There" and a host of other splendid fifties standards. Popped up in only the occasional film, like *White Christmas* (1954). Mother of actor Miguel Ferrer, by then-husband Jose. She is also the aunt of actor George Clooney, son of brother Nick. (*Ted Allan/MPTV*)

A few "notes" from Rosemary Clooney—

"I was told that I started singing even before I talked—I'm not sure of that. But I do know I don't have a singing habit; Bing (Crosby) used to sing here and there—in his house, at a party—not to perform, just because it was part of who he was. Singing has never been a part of me that way (except I do sing when I am putting on makeup for a show—I guess it comes out of me when I know I am about to perform).

I began singing professionally out of necessity; my sister and I were all alone and needed the work. We auditioned at the local radio station with three songs and no music—I didn't know you were supposed to bring it with you—but still got the job, starting at $25 a week.

I enjoy singing—it's what I've done the longest—and would miss it if it went away, but my family is what is really important to me."

"If you live long enough you hear a lot of music—I've been exposed to my own, my children's, and my grandchildren's. My background taught me you had three minutes to tell a story with a song—today things are expressed differently—I prefer the words."

"I know the bad times send you into good reasons for changing. I am happy with the way things are going. I do the best I can."

P E G G Y   L E E
Norma Deloris Engstrom
Born May 16, 1920, in Jamestown, North Dakota
Blessed with a velvety-smooth singing voice, Lee enjoyed worldwide popularity, first as a band singer (most famously with Benny Goodman), then as a performer in nightclubs, television, and far too few films (five to be exact). Oscar-nominated for her role in *Pete Kelly's Blues* (1955), Lee proved a formidable foe for the Disney Organization when she successfully won a suit against them for royalties due her from her work on the animated classic *Lady and the Tramp* (1955). Grammy winner for her poignant recording "Is That All There Is?" in 1969, after thirty-plus years of music hits. Another of her all-time best songs: 1958's "Fever." (*Ted Allan/MPTV*)

left, top
PETULA CLARK
Born November 15, 1932, in Epsom, England
As a child, Clark appeared in many British-made films during and after WWII. She then became a popular singer on the European continent. By the sixties, her popularity spread westward, with finger-popping hits like "Downtown," "I Know a Place" (for which she won a Grammy), "My Love," and "Don't Sleep in the Subway." This enormous acclaim led her to television and back into films, *Finian's Rainbow* (1968) and the musical version of *Goodbye, Mr. Chips* (1969). Unfortunately, neither film proved a boon to her acting career. (*Photofest*)

left, middle
CONNIE FRANCIS
Concetta Rosa Maria Franconero
Born December 12, 1938, in Newark, New Jersey
One of the most popular recording artists of all time, diminutive Connie first gained national attention as winner on "Arthur Godfrey's Talent Scouts" show in 1951. A powerhouse singer, whose massive string of hits, starting with "Who's Sorry Now" (1958), would last only until the mid-'60s. A handful of films, including a personal fave "Where the Boys Are" (1960) failed to properly utilize her comedic talents. Years later, after a much-publicized rape, the loss of her singing voice, and subsequent mental depression, Francis has rebounded, albeit to more manageable public attention and scrutiny. (*Photofest*)

left, bottom
OLIVIA NEWTON-JOHN
Born September 26, 1948, in Cambridge, England
Despite her massive smash with the musical film *Grease* (1978), Olivia did not find continued success in films. Though it hardly mattered. With over a decade of amassing music hits, including "Have You Never Been Mellow" (1975) and "Physical" (the biggest single of 1981), Olivia easily became one of the most popular female singers of the rock era. recently stricken with breast cancer, this grand-daughter of a Nobel Prize–winning physicist, battled back and won the fight. (*Curt Gunther/MPTV*)

right
VANESSA WILLIAMS
Born March 18, 1963, in Tarrytown, New York
If anyone has all the "right stuff," it's this gorgeous woman. She can sing, dance, act, *and* speak her mind. From her meteoric rise to fame as the first Black Miss America (in 1983) and the scandal that marred it; to her rising, phoenix-like, to become a pop diva, Broadway star, renowned actress, and full-time mother. She is an example to us all, women and men, of what we can accomplish even given the most daunting circumstances. (*Kevyn Aucoin*)

"I always knew I wanted to be on the stage, and a dancer—I knew I wanted to dance with Alvin Ailey—and be a theater actress. When I was nine I put together a school production of *The Trojan Horse* and played Electra—I wanted to do everything."

"I had been asked to participate [in the Miss America pageant] a number of times, but wasn't interested. Coming from New York (and the theater), those things were not taken very seriously.—I felt like an outsider; it was this whole system. But I was so surprised that (Miss America) was so 'mom and pop'; it had none of the slickness or corporate participation that the other big pageants had. I remember one of my costumes being made by a pageant director, and one of our chaperones was a contestant's mother.—I was fascinated by the women who made a career out of entering pageants; they would go from state to state hoping for a better chance to win. When I entered, it was more of a fluke, and I gravitated to the other 'first-timers.'"

"I thought, 'this is 1983 and there are armed guards outside my door because someone has threatened to shoot me.'—It hurt to get flack from black people who felt I wasn't black enough.—On one side I was vilified as this scandalous woman, on the other, they were trying to pass me off as a 'Mary Poppins' type—I was a woman in the middle with my own mind and opinions."

"I do not seek out fame; I am much more interested in the quality of my work.—Freedom of choice means a lot to me; I would hate to be just *one* thing. —When you feel trapped you feel sick and miserable—if it isn't working out, move on."

left
MARY MARTIN

Born December 1, 1913, in Weatherford, Texas. Died 1990

A great star of the American stage musical, Martin was also a light-hearted screen actress in several musical films during the early forties. However, it is likely that she will be remembered as Nellie Fornbush (in *South Pacific*), Maria (in *The Sound of Music*) and Peter (in *Peter Pan*); three roles that secure her a place in the annals of Broadway history. Additionally, each role snared her a Tony, including a fourth for her touring part in *Annie Get Your Gun*. She also won an Emmy for her magical reprisal of Pan on television in 1955. Her son is actor Larry Hagman ("I Dream of Jeannie"/"Dallas"). (*Photofest*)

right
CAROL CHANNING

Born January 31, 1921, in Seattle, Washington

Effervescent star, mostly of Broadway and a handful of films. The original Lorelei Lee from *Gentlemen Prefer Blondes*, with her trademark song, "Diamonds Are a Girl's Best Friend." Few individuals have ever come as close to defining true stage presence as this glittering gal (or have lasted as long). A surprising Oscar nominee for her supporting role in 1967's *Thoroughly Modern Millie*. Winner of the 1964 Tony Award for Jerry Herman's *Hello, Dolly!* (winning against Barbra Streisand in *Funny Girl*, no less) in the lead role and what would become a career juggernaut. (By the time she brought a revival of the show back to The Great White Way in the mid-'90s, she had performed the part thousands of times.) (*Wallace Seawell/MPTV*)

HELEN HAYES

Born October 10, 1900, in Washington, D.C. Died 1993

Though she would win two Oscars, for *The Sin of Madelon Claudet* (1931, as Best Actress) and *Airport* (1970, as Best Supporting Actress) after appearing in only a handful of films, Hayes always felt uncomfortable as a film star, choosing instead a life in the theater. (Not typically pretty, she also felt ill-equipped physically for cinema stardom.) It is no surprise then that this gifted thespian would eventually be referred to as our "First Lady of the American Theater." (By her seventies she would also tire of the stage; aggravated by an asthmatic condition.) She has had two theaters named in her honor (the first was demolished in 1982); written six memoirs; had a gold coin struck in her image; been the recipient of an Emmy and two Tonys; and been awarded the National Medal of the Arts in 1988. (*Kobal*)

KATHARINE HEPBURN

Born November 9, 1907, in Hartford, Connecticutt

For someone once (inappropriately) labelled "box office poison," this Bryn Mawr–educated actress has had remarkable success with the medium (including a record twelve Oscar noms with four wins—*Morning Glory* (1933), *Guess Who's Coming to Dinner* (1967), *The Lion in Winter* (1968), and *On Golden Pond* (1981). Long-necked and bony-jointed, she was never the typical-looking Hollywood female, and her indifference to publicity and promotion is legendary. But because of the respect her work commanded, even a twenty-five year intimate relationship with a married Spencer Tracy (starting with their first film (1941's *Woman of the Year*) through eight more, until his death in 1967) was never scandalized by Hollywood journalists. Even an obvious decline in her health (which became visible to the public by the late-'60s) did little to slow down this indomitable Yankee. An Emmy winner, too (as if she had the shelf space), this notorious awards ceremony "no-show" did appear once at the Oscars to present a special award to friend Laurence Weingarten in 1973. (*Author's collection*)

actress

near right, top

VIVIEN LEIGH

Vivian Mary Hartley
Born November 5, 1913, in Darjeeling, India. Died 1967
Leigh came to worldwide attention as the actress chosen to
play Scarlett O'Hara in Selznick's blockbuster *Gone With the
Wind* (1939). This was no small achievement; "Scarlett" was
(and probably still stands as) the most coveted female part in
Hollywood history. But a delicate Leigh, then already romantically linked to Laurence Olivier (married 1940–60), proved
a masterful choice; winning numerous awards for her performance, including an Oscar. Though chronic illness would slow
Leigh throughout her life, it was, ironically, her onscreen (and
stage) physical frailty that so enamored her to audiences,
especially so in her second Oscar-winning role, as Blanche
DuBois in *A Streetcar Named Desire* (1951). Tony winner for
Tovarich (1963). (*Kobal*)

near right, bottom

ANGELA LANSBURY

Born October 16, 1925, in London, England
It was during the war that a young Lansbury came to the
States to continue her dramatic studies. Her first screen
appearance, in *Gaslight* (1944), won great acclaim and her
first (of three) Oscar nominations. Whether it was due to
her acting ability or how she photographed on film, Lansbury
would often play characters far older than she really was,
most notably as Laurence Harvey's mother in *The Manchurian
Candidate* (1962, AAN); she was only three years older than
he was. This flexibility allowed her a great range of roles,
however to today's audiences she is probably known more
for her role as Jessica Fletcher in television's twelve-year
mystery series, "Murder, She Wrote" (1984–96). Though she
would never win the Oscar or the Emmy (despite a near-
record sixteen nominations), some rectification came with
her quad of Tony awards, including one for *Mame* (1966) and
one for *Sweeney Todd* (1979). (*Kobal*)

far right

TALLULAH BANKHEAD

Born January 31, 1903, in Huntsville, Alabama. Died 1968
Legendary stage and too infrequent screen actress and all
around bon vivant. Gloriously beautiful to behold with a
memorable throaty drawl, Tallulah led a scandalous life
almost from the moment she left the protection of her
Speaker of the House father, William Bronkman Bankhead.
Even rumors of bisexuality could not impede her, although
Hollywood found little to showcase this dynamic and tem-
pestuous performer. Possibly her best film work was in
Hitchcock's *Lifeboat* (1944), a role that won her the New
York Film Critics Best Actress award, but was surprisingly
overlooked by the Academy. Hmmm. Two of her best (and
most cited) quotes, among dozens: "I am as pure as the dri-
ven slush," and "Cocaine isn't habit forming. I should know—
I've been using it for years." (*Kobal*)

above

E L E A N O R　P A R K E R

Born June 26, 1922, in Cedarville, Ohio
Though nominated for three Oscars (*Caged*, 1950; *Detective Story*, 1951; *Interrupted Melody*, 1955), Parker is probably best known to contemporary audiences as the "Countess" in *The Sound of Music* (Best Picture, 1965). Nevertheless, throughout the forties and fifties she was a major star, as well regarded for her acting as she was for her refined beauty. (*Richard Miller/MPTV*)

near right, top

O L I V I A　D E　H A V I L L A N D

Born July 1, 1916 in Tokyo, Japan
Early roles as the damsel-in-distress, to some of the screen's highest caliber work (and estranged sister to fellow thespian Joan Fontaine), Olivia is also very much responsible for establishing a star's rights to their own career (by fighting a hard-won battle with Warner Bros. to limit a contract's length, in the mid-'40s). Multi-Oscar nominated and two-time winner (*To Each His Own*, 1946, and her standout role as *The Heiress*, 1948). During the height of her career, she left films (for the most part) and went to the theater. By the mid '50s she moved to Paris, the city this fair beauty still calls home. (*Paul Hesse/MPTV*)

near right, middle

J E A N　S I M M O N S

Born January 31, 1929, in London, England
Delicate, dark-featured beauty, who proved quite a formidable talent—before turning twenty—in a group of literate, British-made films, including *Great Expectations* (1946), *Black Narcissus* (1947), and Olivier's *Hamlet* (1948), for which she was nominated for an Oscar. In 1950, she married and came stateside with actor Stewart Granger (they would divorce in 1960). However, Simmons did not begin work until 1953, wherein she became a bonafide American star with *The Robe*, *The Actress*, etc. In 1960, she married author/director Richard Brooks and was cast in his melodrama *Elmer Gantry*. She continued to work through the sixties, capping off the decade with another Oscar nom for *The Happy Ending* (1969). Emmy-winner for the television mini-series "The Thorn Birds" (1983). (*Paul Hesse/MPTV*)

far right

P A T R I C I A　N E A L

Born January 20, 1926, in Packard, Kentucky
Northwestern University–educated, Neal began as a model then graduated to the stage. Eventually, the Tony-winning thespian would find her way to Hollywood and great early notices, as in the almost surreal *Fountainhead* (1949) opposite Gary Cooper (with whom she was linked offscreen) and *The Day the Earth Stood Still* (1951). In 1953 she married author Roald Dahl and did not return to the screen for four years, when she appeared in Kazan's *A Face in the Crowd*. The next few years saw her in *Breakfast at Tiffany's* (1962) and her Oscar-winner *Hud* (1963). In 1965, a debilitating stroke left her semiparalyzed and without cognitive speech. Fighting through these maladies, which befell her during a fifth pregnancy, she returned triumphantly to the screen in *The Subject Was Roses* (1968, AAN). She has also had to endure the death of a daughter, the severe injury of one of her boys, a nervous breakdown, and divorce from her devoted husband (he was having an affair with one of her best friends). Few actresses have had to endure such catastrophic circumstances and still accomplish such well-regarded careers. (*Kobal*)

left

J O A N N E   W O O D W A R D
Born February 27, 1930, in Thomasville, Georgia
A most versatile and capable film thespian, which she proved without question with her Oscar-winning performance (which could be counted as a trio of roles) in *The Three Faces of Eve* (1957). She has since been nominated three more times, for *Rachel, Rachel* (1968), *Summer Wishes, Winter Dreams* (1973), and *Mr. and Mrs. Bridge* (1990). The latter was with her husband (since 1958), Paul Newman, with whom she has appeared on a number of previous occasions, including in the steamy *Long, Hot Summer* (1958) and *From the Terrace* (1960). A well-loved and respected bigtime Hollywood liberal, Woodward also has two Emmys that were added to her collection for the tele-flicks *See How She Runs* (1978) and *Do You Remember Love?* (1985). (*Corbis-Bettmann*)

right

A N N E   B A N C R O F T
A n n a   M a r i a   L o u i s e   I t a l i a n o
Born September 17, 1931, in the Bronx, NY
Like so many before and since, the early promotion of Bancroft as a sexy starlet was not uncommon. Not surprisingly, success would elude her this first time out. However, these initial screen roles are a remarkable counter to the dramatic crescendoes Bancroft would be lauded for in just a few short years. A trip to Broadway resulted in back-to-back professional triumphs; the first, a Tony for her role opposite Henry Fonda in *Two For a Seesaw* (1958), which was followed by the role that would make her a sensation, as Annie Sullivan in *The Miracle Worker*. This Tony award–winning role led her back to Hollywood and the screen version, and the Oscar. One of filmdom's most reliable performers, Bancroft has won plaudits (and Oscar nominations) for *The Pumpkin Eater* (1964), *The Turning Point* (1977), and *Agnes of God* (1985). But in this author's humble opinion, her finest work was as the lascivious, bitch-mother, Mrs. Robinson, in Mike Nichols' *The Graduate* (1967). What a fabulous wardrobe, too! Married since 1964 to comedian/producer/actor Mel Brooks. (*Archive Photos*)

"There is nothing as honest as the 'contract' between an actor and the audience. It says, 'The audience will suspend disbelief for this amount of time and allow you (the actor) to be who you tell them you are going to be and will represent to the best of your ability.' I wish all agreements were as straightforward as that."

"On stage, you find yourself concerned with projecting your voice and the physical relationship you have with the live audience. When acting on film, the medium allows you to go deeper into a character and reveal more subtlety and complexity."

"You don't realize what you can do until someone believes in you or gives you encouragement. When you are around a crowd of people, don't you find yourself talking more to the person who laughs at your jokes than to the ones who don't?"

"I think writers may have the hardest job—they start out with a blank piece of paper.—Without good writing, you begin to see how powerless you are as an actor and your work can suffer.—I think a lot of today's best writers have been curtailed; they act as self-censors, thinking they'll be rejected, and step away from something even before they begin."

Gena Rowlands

GENA ROWLANDS

Born June 19, 1934, in Cambria, Wisconsin

Often actors start out playing one type of role and end up being wholly thought of in another way. This gifted thespian, noted for her natural acting style, surprisingly began her career as a "dreamgirl" in *The Seven Year Itch*. Soon after, her talents led to Hollywood. However, it would be her appearances in husband John Cassavetes' films that Gena's career really took hold. Improvised and gritty, his movies provided the perfect backdrop for her complex characterizations. Their work together resulted in her two Best Actress nominations, for *A Woman Under the Influence* (1974) and *Gloria* (1980). Two-time Emmy winner, one for her title role in *The Betty Ford Story* (1987). Mother of director Nick Cassavetes. (*Corbis-Bettmann*)

INGRID BERGMAN

Born August 29, 1915. Died 1982

It seems strange with today's loosened morals that there was a time (and not so long ago) when what a person did in their personal life could actually restrict what they did professionally. Such were the circumstances surrounding Bergman, back in the late-'40s. Ingrid enjoyed worldwide fame and success as an acclaimed actress, almost from the moment of her American screen debut in 1939. Her wholesome and luminous, near angelic presence, was applauded in films from *Casablanca* to *Gaslight* (the latter, her first of three Oscar winners). Then, in what was taken as a betrayal to her fans, Ingrid became smitten with director Roberto Rossellini while still married to Dr. Peter Lindstrom. Choosing the course of true love, Bergman "deserted" her husband and daughter, Pia, for Rossellini. This caused such an uproar that even the U.S. Senate, along with religious groups and the like, asked that she be barred from filmmaking. So, for the next seven years she was effectively exiled. But Hollywood and American film audiences eventually "forgave" her indiscretions, and her first major film release in years, *Anastasia* (1956), won her an Academy Award. A nice welcome back. Her final Oscar came for a memorable supporting turn in 1974's *Murder on the Orient Express*. (*Archive Photos*)

MERYL STREEP

Born 1951, in Basking Ridge, New Jersey With a near-record eleven Oscar nominations, Streep is unquestionably the most-lauded actress working in films today. Her serene good looks are often in contrast (though frequently quite complementary) to her remarkable ability to tackle deeply dramatic (and, too infrequently, comedic) roles. She, like few actresses before her or since, has the ability to transcend her material, making the vast majority of her films notable (and watchable) just by her mere presence. And her amazingly changeable dialect makes these appearances equally listenable. First nominated for *The Deer Hunter* (1978). First Oscar for *Kramer Vs. Kramer* (1979), second for *Sophie's Choice* (1981). Also an Emmy-winner for the TV miniseries "Holocaust" (1978). (*Brian Aris/Corbis-Outline*)

right

BETTE DAVIS

Ruth Elizabeth Davis Born April 5, 1908, in Lowell, Massachusetts. Died 1989 The first lady of the American screen. In the beginning, Davis' career was strewn with so much negativity it's a wonder she chose to continue in a business that didn't seem to want her. But her indomitable spirit persevered, and through role after role, began to amass a body of work unequaled in filmdom. By the mid-thirties, a hard-nosed Davis emerged, one who fought for better roles (even though she lost the actual battle, she seemed to have won the war). *Of Human Bondage* (1934) and *Dangerous* (1935, her first Oscar winner) are early standouts. By the forties, her mannered yet memorable acting style was in place and her output of Warner Bros, "women's pictures" were pure gold. In terms of quality and numbers, no actress can touch them. Watch *Now, Voyager* and *Little Foxes* if you are in doubt. A career setback in the late forties was met with a triumphant return in *All About Eve* (Best Picture, 1950). In the early sixties, she was called upon to resurrect her career again with a magnificently slovenly portrayal in *Whatever Happened to Baby Jane?* (1962). It became her tenth Oscar nomination, winning two (the second was for 1938's *Jezebel*). Also an Emmy winner, Bette was a star of the highest order; strange when you consider she was initially never thought of as star material or particularly attractive. She even memorably referred to herself as one of the few whom Hollywood allowed to "come out of the water looking wet." A fighter to the end, it is not likely we will see a repeat performance of her kind again. (*MPTV*)

BETTE DAVIS

MODERN SCREEN

JANUARY
10
CENTS

Scoop! INTIMATE **LOVE LETTERS** OF THE STARS

What struck me as most surprising when I spoke with Liza was her way of making a person feel like an old friend, even if it was their very first meeting (or talk). She has a way of engaging the other person that makes you know she's as interested in what you have to say as her own responses. This form of gracious interaction was not lost on me — it is rare to feel it coming from any person, celebrity or not.

She tells me that from the start *movement* was what interested her. "I had all this energy, and I loved music," she said. How great it must have been to be where (and who) she was. Well, not really, she noted, "It was not fascinating for a kid to watch a movie being made. In fact, movies in general held no fascination — everyone in town made them. All of my parents' friends were in the business — it was work." Which is why she chose to go into theater first, it meant "freedom." But the company of her parents and their cronies did have a positive effect (to say the least), "I was surrounded by great artists — directors, writers, actors. My parents were considered Hollywood 'intelligentsia,' they attracted terribly talented people. My appreciation for great talent comes from them." And because of their influence and her own renowned gifts she certainly knows what to look for from an actor. "A good performance is solid, it moves and creates a world that is not spare parts." She also knows what to expect of oneself, when performing. "Always look at it from the point of view of the audience; what would they like?"

When you are the daughter of Judy Garland and Vincente Minnelli, your life is pretty much destined to be an open book; the exposure has not dulled her enthusiasm for life. Amazingly, her loss of privacy was never an issue, because she says she never knew what it was like to miss it. However, she touchingly adds, "The feelings are the same, only the facts are different."

The fact that she treats her own immense talent as a gift she willingly gives to others is an incredible act of generosity, and we are fortunate to see it when given the opportunity. I had always assumed she treated it this way because she still manages to come out on top, no matter the trials and tribulations she has borne. But her own summation is more honest, heart-felt, and to the point, "Strive, hope, and believe — and more than anything, always be grateful."

entertainer

DEBBIE REYNOLDS
Mary Frances Reynolds
Born April 1, 1932, in El Paso, Texas
An unsinkable Hollywood favorite. Few have the drive or the talent to match this one-woman entertainment bonanza. Starting with Warner Bros., then moving to MGM, she was the darling of a slew of toe-tapping musicals throughout the fifties, including the priceless *Singin' in the Rain* (1952). Her career was at the height of its popularity during the late fifties and early sixties; she showed a great flair for drama (*The Rat Race*, 1960) and received an Oscar nomination for *The Unsinkable Molly Brown* (1963). By the seventies, with family fare on the wane, she ably turned to the stage, and for the duration of the eighties and into the nineties she did not appear in any feature films. But like the indefatigable force we knew her to be, Reynolds reemerged in the last few years as a sublime character actress, in both movies (*Mother*, 1996) and episodic television ("Will and Grace," 1999). Once infamously married to singer Eddie Fisher (ending via his relationship with their friend, Elizabeth Taylor). Mother of writer Carrie Fisher, and an important early anti-smoking advocate.
(*Corbis-Bettmann*)

SHIRLEY MACLAINE

Born April 24, 1934, in Richmond, Virginia Shirley (the older sister of actor Warren Beatty) got her big break by playing understudy to Carol Haney in the Broadway musical, *The Pajama Game*. The story goes, Haney injured herself shortly after the opening and MacLaine was called in to replace her; that night producer Hal Wallis was in the audience—he immediately signed her to a movie contract. To her credit, MacLaine's "overnight" success began with her first public appearance at age four and lasted well through her many screen incarnations (resulting in five Oscar noms and one win, for *Terms of Endearment* [1983]). Whether playing the hooker with a heart of gold (*Sweet Charity*, 1969) or an alleged lesbian (*The Children's Hour*, 1963), MacLaine's diverse career highlights, which have included nightclubs, television, and writing, could be attributed to her renowned belief in reincarnation, or just plain talent. (*Corbis-Bettmann*)

BARBRA STREISAND

Born April 24, 1942, in Brooklyn, New York Gifted, multitalented maverick entertainer. Streisand did not become a star necessarily overnight, although it seems that way. Even though her Broadway debut (in *I Can Get it For You Wholesale*, 1962) made her the toast-of-the-town, she struggled to reach that moment. However, soon thereafter, few could match her meteoric rise. A savvy CBS snapped her up after her appearance in the stage musical *Funny Girl*, and led her quickly to television (two Emmys) and recording success (two Grammys). With her 1968 film recreation of her role as Fanny Brice in *Funny Girl*, she added movie stardom to her list of accomplishments (and the first of her two Oscars; the second was for cowriting the song, "Evergreen," for *A Star is Born*, 1976). Through the seventies, she was a top box-office draw. In 1983, she turned ably to directing, beginning with *Yentl*, and became a leader in a field unfairly dominated by men. Only recently has she been performing again live, including a concert appearance to honor President Clinton. Now, famously married to actor James Brolin, her second. (*Corbis-Bettmann*)

left

DIANA ROSS
Diane Earle
Born March 26, 1944, in Detroit, Michigan
Even when she was topping the charts with the Supremes in the 1960s, anyone could see she was destined for far greater recognition. Her talent was palpable, and her sex appeal, inescapable. By the time the top-selling "girl" group lost their lead singer in 1970, Ross was already on her way to legendary status. As a soloist her career took off, just as expected. When she added acting to the mix, she went on to even more acclaim (and an Oscar nomination, for 1972's *Lady Sings the Blues*, her first time out). If she disappoints, it's because we don't see or hear her often enough. (*Wallace Seawell/MPTV*)

right

JULIE ANDREWS
Julia Elizabeth Wells
Born Oct. 1, 1935, in Walton-on-Thames, England
A most "loverly" lady, Andrews began singing (on the radio) in childhood. Was one of the few (monstrously) successful musical stars to come out of the 1960s, well after the genre's Golden Age. Married first to set designer Tony Walton, now to director Blake Edwards (since 1968), with whom she has worked frequently. Films include her Oscar-winning *Mary Poppins* (1964), released the same year she was passed over to recreate her acclaimed Eliza Doolittle in the cinematic version of *My Fair Lady*—for the more "bankable" Audrey Hepburn; *The Sound of Music* (1965, another Oscar nom); and *Victor/Victoria* (1982, her most recent Oscar nomination). (*Bob Willoughby/MPTV*)

M A D O N N A
Madonna Louise Veronica Ciccone
Born August 16, 1958, in Bay City, Michigan
Unarguably, one of the most influential entertainers (female or male) of the entire century. Half of Madonna's appeal lies in an uncanny ability to satisfy (and grow) with an enormous worldwide audience. Starting with playful dance-pop ditties like "Everybody" in 1983 and her big breakout "Like a Virgin" (1984), through innumerable music and non-music successes, to her recent Grammy-winning smash cd, *Ray of Light* (1998), the evidence is clear. Obviously, the other half of the attraction stems from her uniquely candid and likeable personality. (It also helps that she's a "hottie," too!) Her often controversial outlook on life pushes the envelope (and a lot of people's buttons), but one thing is certain: with her you know where you stand. Perplexingly, it seems films may be the only endeavor, as yet, where Madonna hasn't reigned supreme, though a recent Golden Globe win for *Evita* (1996) shows her enormous potential. Without doubt, Madonna will work this out to her (and her fan's) satisfaction when the time (and the right vehicles) come along. (*David LaChapelle/Outline*)

As you can imagine, it takes a lot of (patient and generous) people to put together a book; this humble effort was no exception. Therefore, the author would like to graciously extend his heartfelt thanks and appreciation to the following organizations and individuals, without whom *Heavenly* could not exist:

First, to my unflappable editor Abigail Wilentz, whose support of the project was unquestioned even when there was doubt among others. You are a bloom in the desert. And to the entire staff at **Universe**, from Bonnie Eldon, John Brancati, Dan Tucker, Robin Key, Michael Patterson, to publisher Charles Miers, who together manage to produce the most beautiful things under the most chaotic of circumstances; I am in awe. To Jed Root, for forgoing his better instincts and making it possible to do what I felt I needed to be done. Thank you. And to his company, **Jed Root, Inc.**, for their able and unquestioned support. To Pascal Dangin, whose amazing artistry often goes unmentioned and his entire crew at **Box**, thank you for rescuing me.

To my longtime pals Joe and Dan; Tony (whose whole life's love of "most" of the women herein was a great part of my inspiration); Miisa and Lee (and their newborns); Teresa; Lou; Mark (though we don't see each other enough); Darlene and John, and Chris (a new West Coast addition); Chicagoland's finest, Jeff (forever) and Eddie, Peter and John; Greg; Jim and Gary; Wayne; Philly's best, Mitch and Harris; Joyce (a one-woman fan club); Vicky (I tried, but the "Queen" didn't fit); Boston fave's Mike and Chris; Eric; and finally, to Kevyn, whose generosity, support, and enthusiasm showed me the strength of our friendship, which was there all along. To my Dad, brother Len, brother-in-law Tom, and nephew Prescott, but most notably to Mom and sister Janet, who influenced the contents of this book, whether they knew it or not. Also, to Red (and his cohorts), you guys get me through these things. And last but not least, to Robert, who technically doesn't qualify for *Heavenly*, at least not in book form. You are my anchor and my best friend, I don't know what I'd do without you but wouldn't want to try.

And because necessary lists can be so much fun to play with: genial Gina Avery, the ever benevolent Geoffrey Beene, Esme Chandlee, sexy Bob Cosenza and the entire staff at **Kobal**, the delightful Donna Daley, noble Norman Curry, victorious Victor Hotho, and the entire staff at **Corbis-Bettmann**, magnificent Meryl Delierre and the entire staff at **Everett**, Margie Duncan, Andrew Eccles, Marcy Engelman, **The Flower Shop**, Gary Fuchs, Phil Gersh, Dr. Leonard Gordon, lovely Yen Graney and the entire staff at **MPTV Archives**, Richard Grant, lucky Leon Hall, Jane Halsman, "studboy" Jim Johnson (yeah, baby!), Deborah Kellerman, "hunkasaraus" Mark Kerrigan and the entire staff at **Celebrity Services**, Kristi Kittendorf, randy Ron Knoth, Jeffrey Lane, luscious Laurie Lion at **Corbis-Outline**, jovial John Lum and the entire staff at **ComZone**, cuddly Kevin Mancuso, hot Howard Mendelbaum and the entire staff at **Photofest**, Wendy Morris, "cut-up" Cathy Mouton and the entire staff at **Linda Dozoretz**, playful Peter Rohowsky and sassy Arlete Santos, and the entire staff at **Archive Photos**, Sheldon Roskin, Marge Schictanz, Kitt Shapiro, Alan Spiritoff, everyone at **Trade, Inc.**, Christine Tripicchio, Jean-Marc Vlaminck, winsome Julia Winston, **Wolf-Kasteler**, and Gene Yusem, thank you one and all.

The following publications were used as reference materials for *Heavenly*:

Halliwell's Filmgoer's Companion (Twelfth Edition)
Total Television: The Comprehensive Guide to Programming from Past to Present by A. McNeil
The Film Lover's Companion edited by David Quinlan
The Film Encyclopedia by Ephraim Katz
The Big Book of Show Business Awards by David Sheward
The Billboard Book of Top-40 Hits (Sixth Edition) by Joel Whitburn

acknowledgments

right
ANN BLYTH
Born August 28, 1928, in Mt. Kisco, New York
Though she has a trained singing voice, put to some good use in a spate of musicals (*The Great Caruso*, 1951, and *Kismet*, 1955), Blyth will probably best be remembered for two widely disparate career moments: acting for many years as a commercial spokesperson for a famed baked-goods company, and as the spiteful, spoiled daughter-from-hell of Joan Crawford, Vita, in *Mildred Pierce* (1945). This screen characterization garnered her an Oscar nomination and many an ardent follower; she was spectacular. (*Archive Photos*)

closing page
CAROL LYNLEY
Carolyn Lee
Born February 13, 1942, in New York City, NY
Like so many bright and promising actresses, Lynley may have been lost in the shuffle that surrounds a profusion of equally talented (or not) hungry starlets and not enough adequate film roles to go around. However, Carol did show quite capable skills when she played the lead in one of two biopics of actress Jean Harlow (*Harlow*, 1965), and in *Bunny Lake is Missing* (that same year, for Otto Preminger). (*Corbis-Bettmann*)

endpapers, left to right
SYLVIA SIDNEY
Sophia Kosow
Born August 8, 1910. in the Bronx, NY. Died 1999

MIRIAM HOPKINS
Born October 18, 1902, in Bainbridge, Ga. Died 1972

Two of the best actresses of their day. Sidney excelled at playing the angelic waif while Hopkins made her mark as an acid-tongued bitch. Both careers faltered after early stardom, only to re-emerge as noted character players. Sidney was Oscar-nominated for Best Supporting Actress in 1971 for *Summer Wishes, Winter Dreams*, Hopkins for Best Actress for *Becky Sharp* (1935). (*Everett Collection*)

back cover
NANETTE FABRAY
Ruby Bernadette Nanette Fabares
Born October 27, 1920, in San Diego, California
An Emmy (two times for "Caesar's Hour") and Tony award—winner, who is best known to today's audiences for playing episodic television moms (*One Day At a Time*), instead of for the musical-comedy talents that made her a star. (Tune into 1953's *The Bandwagon* the next time it plays on television.) A President's Distinguished Service Award winner, she was also a featured child-actress in many "Our Gang" serials of the late-'20s. (*Kobal*)